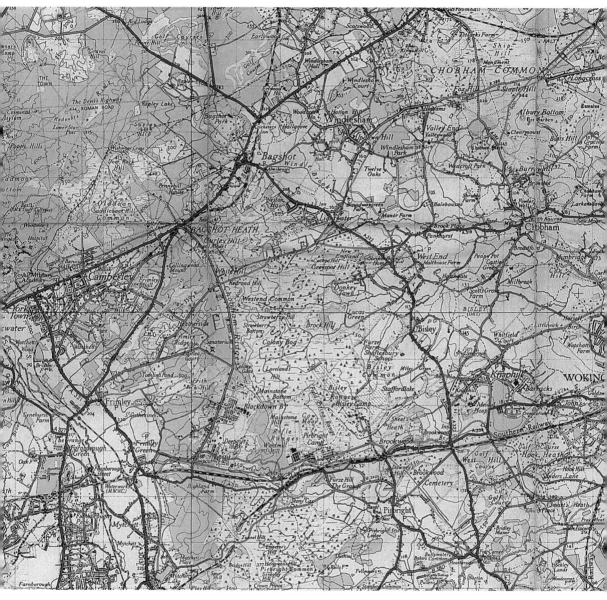

Map of Surrey Heath, based on the O.S. 2 inch map of 1940

LIFE AND WORK ON SURREY HEATH

Mary Ann Bennett

Phillimore

2007

Published by
PHILLIMORE AND CO. LTD,
Chichester, West Sussex, PO20 2DD

ISBN 978-1-86077-492-8

Printed and bound in Great Britain

CONTENTS

LIST OF ILLUSTRATIONS

Frontispiece - Map of Surrey Heath, based on the O.S. 2 in map of 1940
xii - Geology map of Surrey Heath

ACKNOWLEDGEMENTS

The author would like to thank the staff at Surrey History Centre, Hampshire Record Office and the Museum of English Rural Life at Reading for all the assistance given to her. She would also like to thank the following: Harry Goold and Mrs Margery Dowling for allowing her to copy extracts from the diary of their Uncle, Frederick Street, and for the loan of family photographs; Mr and Mrs Bert Saunders for allowing her to photograph their gypsy van; Mr Richard Wilson for allowing her to quote from his articles in *Home Words* and for the use of his drawings and family photographs; Peter Fuller, Ernie Wells, Bill Godfrey, Brian Berry, Arthur Glazier, Harry Goold and Peter Higgs for permission to quote from their reminiscences; Anthony Greenstreet for allowing her to quote from his articles; Mr and Mrs Brian Cole for their kind permission to use the photograph of William and Mary Cole and for information regarding their family; Mrs Kathleen Burgess for sharing her knowledge of the nurseries and gardens; to Mr Burrows for allowing me to copy deeds held by the family; to Sharon Cross, Curator of Surrey Heath Museum, for allowing copies of photographs within the Museum collection to be reproduced.

The author would also like to thank the following for permission to use copies of their photos held at the Museum and in private collections: Mrs Kathleen Alexander, Mr A. Attewell, Mr Graham Barson, the late Mr Frederick Benham and his daughter Phyllis Benham, Mr Brian Berry, Mr M. Clift, Mr and Mrs Robin Daborn, Mrs P. Davis, Mr Vic Deeks, Mr John End, Mrs Sylvia Greeno, Mr David Howcroft, Mr and Mrs William Donald, Mr William Godfrey, the late Miss Barbara Hall, Mr Mike Hawley, Mr Peter Higgs, the late Mr John Jillings, Mrs Leech, the late Mr Mansfield, Mr Malcolm Miller, Mr and Mrs Pain, Mr F. Penhallow, Mrs P. Phillips, Mrs Bunty Richings, the late Miss Ida Salt, the late Mr James Scott, the late Mrs Mary Sheffield, Mr Colin Sinnott, Mrs Smith, Mr Alf Tarry, Mrs Heather Toynbee, Mrs Joan Weymouth and Mrs Olive Wright.

She is also grateful to Graham Barson, Phil Stevens and Eamon Ryan for proof-reading the text and for making amendments and suggestions regarding the content of the book. Also to Phil Stevens for translating the Frimley Manorial Court records from Latin to English.

ILLUSTRATION
ACKNOWLEDGEMENTS

Frontispiece – James Rutter
xii – H.G. Dines and F.H. Edmunds (1924)/Surrey Heath Museum

Alexander Collection/Surrey Heath Museum, 114; Attewell Collection/Surrey Heath Museum, 113; Barnett Collection/Surrey Heath Museum, 94; Barson Collection/Surrey Heath Museum, 64; Benham Collection/Surrey Heath Museum, 9, 11, 12, 18, 46, 51, 52, 69, 82, 86, 90, 101, 102, 109; Bennett Collection, 71, 72; Berry Collection/Surrey Heath Museum, 130; Camberley Library Collection/Surrey Heath Museum, 62; Chobham Museum Collection/Surrey Heath Museum, 38; Clift, 120; Mr and Mrs Brian Cole, 43; Collins Collection/Surrey Heath Museum, 96; Henry H. Crombie, 49; Daborn Collection/Surrey Heath Museum, 122, 131; Davis Collection/Surrey Heath Museum, 10, 84, 95, 115, 119, 134; Deeks Collection/Surrey Heath Museum, 65; Donald Collection/Surrey Heath Museum, 127; Elkins Collection/Surrey Heath Museum, 30, 99, 116; End Collection/Surrey Heath Museum, 14, 24, 25, 121; Godfrey Collection/Surrey Heath Museum, 128; Goold Collection/Surrey Heath Museum, 124, 126; Greeno Collection/Surrey Heath Museum, 132; Hall Collection/Surrey Heath Museum, 67, 141; Hawley Collection/Surrey Heath Museum, 74; Higgs Collection/Surrey Heath Museum, 129; Howcroft Collection/Surrey Heath Museum, 3, 13, 15, 17, 22, 30, 31, 38, 41, 88, 91, 136; Hughes, G.M., *A History of Windsor Forest Sunninghill and the Great Park* (1890), 45; Jillings Collection/Surrey Heath Museum, 83; Kenner Collection/Surrey Heath Museum, 70; Leech Collection/Surrey Heath Museum, 39; Mansfield Collection/Surrey Heath Museum, 137; Medhurst Card, 52; Miller Collection/Surrey Heath Museum, 4, 138; *Norman's Directory*, 62, 135 (1889); Penhallow Collection/Surrey Heath Museum, 73, 111, 142, 143; Phillips Collection/Surrey Heath Museum, 63; Robert Tucker Pain Collection/Surrey Heath Museum, 2, 6, 16, 25, 89; Rock & Co., 53, 54, 55, 56, 57, 58; Royal Military Academy Sandhurst Collection/Surrey Heath Museum, 34, 80; Richard Lucock Wilson/Surrey Heath Museum, 5, 40, 104; Richings Collection/Surrey Heath Museum, 8, 98; *Sadler & Baker Brochure*, 139, 140, 145; Salt Collection/Surrey Heath Museum, 60; Scott Collection/Surrey Heath Museum, 87, 93, 97; Sheffield Collection/Surrey Heath Museum, 117, 118; Sinnott Collection/Surrey Heath Museum, 68, 79, 133; Smith Collection, 112; Surrey Heath Museum, 7, 19, 20, 21, 22, 23, 32, 33, 35, 36, 42, 44, 47, 48, 59, 62, 66, 75, 77, 78, 81, 85, 92, 100, 103, 105, 106, 107, 108, 125, 123, 144; Tarry Collection, 110; Turner Collection/Surrey Heath Museum, 76; Weymouth Collection/Surrey Heath Museum, 50; Whittle Collection/Surrey Heath Musuem, 27; Wright Collection/Surrey Heath Museum, 1; James Wyld, 48.

INTRODUCTION

The administrative area known today as Surrey Heath was formed in 1974. It is made up of the villages of Chobham, Bisley, Bagshot and Windlesham, part of Sunningdale, Lightwater, West End, Frimley, Frimley Green, Deepcut, Mytchett and Camberley. Historically this north-west corner of Surrey consisted of four villages: Chobham, the largest, with its West End and northern settlements of Burrow Hill and Valley End; Windlesham, predominantly a farming community with its more commercial or trade area of Bagshot; Frimley, the only village to have a resident lord of the manor, with its South End or Frimley Green and far south area known originally as Mitchet; and Bisley, the smallest of the four villages. These settlements were oases of reasonably productive farmland, surrounded by the heathland after which the current borough of Surrey Heath is named; it also shaped the lives of generations of people who lived and worked in the villages. The majority of the residents, then as now, lived in the centre of villages or were farmers. The villages contained the normal trades associated with daily life and the farms produced the same crops and reared the same animals as those all over England. There were, however, constraints and influences, the conjunction of which had a bearing on people's daily lives and the way in which opportunities for much-needed additional work developed. The lack of any large rivers, the nature of the soil and especially the vast acreage of heathland made for an area which was slow to develop, with the few of inhabitants relying on a traditional way of life until the early 19th century when enclosure of the heathland brought change.

Surrey Heath is an area where Barton Beds, Bracklesham Beds and Bagshot Sands predominate. These are only moisture-retentive where small beds of clay or the larger spread of the 'iron pan' hold water. This book attempts to look at all the influences of heathland on the development of Surrey Heath, how and why it became the area it is today, and how the people who lived here managed to make a living from what was generally regarded as 'given up to barrenness, horrid and frightful to look on, not only good for little, but good for nothing'.[1]

There are no large rivers in Surrey Heath and the few slow-flowing streams which pass through the area are barely strong enough to provide the energy for the water-mills that were needed to grind corn for local use; they were certainly not suitable for any other large-scale commercial use. From the 11th century until

Geology map of Surrey Heath in 1924, based on the O.S. map of 1887

1813 the area was within the bounds of the royal hunting forest of Windsor. Life for the population prior to the Enclosure Acts in the early 19th century was centred on small-scale farming with additional income derived from supplementary trades. Local people were both blessed and trammelled by the heathland surrounding their arable land. An example of a local family will be given to highlight the way of life for each trade or source of income where possible. The changes to trade brought about by enclosure of the heathland will also be discussed.

The natural benefits of heathland included: a limited amount of sarsen stone used for churches and the more substantial village houses; clay which supported pottery shops and brickworks; sand and gravel; and turf, which heated their homes and fired their kilns. People were also able to graze their animals on the heath and collect the gorse, heather and broom for use in their farms and homes. The main drawback was the unfailing tendency of the heathland to encroach on any newly improved soil. The prospect of land which could be improved and used for growing crops was one incentive for enclosure. In 1772 the vicar of Windlesham wrote, 'It must be a pain to any man who has ye least degree of feeling for his fellow creatures in distress to see many thousand acres of land capable of producing the necessaries of life an uncultivated desert.'[2]

The villages were fairly isolated, with the exception of Bagshot with its royal residence and the benefits of the turnpike road. With little opportunity for work or for new industry the population remained small until after the arrival of the Basingstoke canal, which brought in coal, the development of the Royal Military College at Sandhurst; and the post-enclosure growth of the nursery industry.

The geology of this area of Surrey is of the Eocene period, with downwash gravels from the Pleistocene period. The borough lies on the north-west edge of the Weald and the southern limits of the London Basin. It is one of the largest areas of Plateau Gravel with an underlying stratum of Barton Beds, Bracklesham Beds and Bagshot Beds. Chobham Ridges are composed of Barton Sand under a layer of Plateau Gravel. Bracklesham Bed outcrops occur on the lowest areas of these ridges under a layer of loamy peat.

The main rivers threading their way through the heathland are the Bourne and the Windlebrook in the east of the borough, and the Blackwater and Wish Steams which form its western boundary. The largest of these is the Bourne and its tributaries.

The heathland was formed when early settlers, Stone Age or Neolithic, cleared the land of trees to establish fields for agriculture. The burning of smaller shrubs and ground cover and the grazing of animals eventually produced a treeless landscape. Settlers would then have moved on leaving this poor land, which became home to the heathland plants we see today.

Chapter One

A FARMING LIFE

COMMON FIELDS AND CHERTSEY ABBEY

Given the nature of the land the farmers were able to do little more than supply their own needs and those of their neighbours. They had an advantage in that, if there were any surplus produc-e, there was a ready market, at Bagshot and the northern edge of Frimley where there were travellers and the hostelries that served them. In summer there were often tented military camps that needed supplies for the horses and men. However, it is unlikely that many local farmers could have had much to spare as it appears they generally had to engage in a second trade to make ends meet. Those who did not have land worked either as day labourers or as farm servants living-in with the family.

As Phil Stevens points out in *Surrey Heath under the Tudor and Stuarts*, local land was not suitable for traditional common strip cultivation as it was gained over the centuries by improving forest and heathland. The land had been held by Chertsey Abbey until the dissolution in the 16th century and the Chertsey Cartularies contain the records of transactions with the farming population. These transactions indicate an area where families worked smallholdings with a few men having a virgate (30 acres) or a half-virgate of land. In addition to their own work farmers were required to shear sheep and plough, mow, reap and carry crops for the abbot at Chertsey.

Although there were common fields in each of the villages they would have been worked communally rather than in strip rotation. In strip rotation usually one third was left for the rough grazing of animals but in Surrey Heath local farmers had the advantage of grazing on the heathland and did not require this benefit. In Frimley any common fields had been extinguished long before the Enclosure Act of 1801 but evidence of communal use of land exists in the field names. Field Lane in Frimley and Bedford Lane in Frimley Green (formerly known as Field Lane) would have led to the common fields. At the end of Field Lane in Frimley was 'Tomlyns', a Saxon name for common heather land. At the end of Bedford Lane was 'Doles' meadow, another name for land used for the poor or communally.

Windlesham had the greatest number of common fields, which were identified as Eastage, Westage, Ashington, Church Field, Down Field and Wood Cut, Thorndown and Bagshot, consisting in total of 156 acres in 1813.[1] In the Chobham manorial

1 *Streets Heath, West End, gorse and heather encroaching*

court records for 1768 several common fields are referred to. These were at North Ditch, Westearsh, Northearsh and, in West End, Cranish and 'the Butt in the Little Common Field'.[2] The common fields at Bisley were quite extensive considering the size of the parish, straddling both sides of the main route to Guildford.

CROPS GROWN AND LIVESTOCK KEPT

The earliest record available of the animals kept and crops grown in Surrey Heath is in Chobham when in 1595 the parishioners' tithe to the vicar included a large variety of goods. Each Good Friday he was entitled to 'tithe eggs', three for every

2 *Carting hay in Frimley, 1870s*

cock kept and two for each hen, or money in lieu. He would gain one tenth of all 'Apples, pearse, plumbs wheresoever they grow in the parish, the tenth of Beans, hashings, roots and hopps … of mustard seed and hemp flax.'[3] He was also entitled to a tenth of a swarm of bees or their produce, the same of each calf, pig or goose, 1s. for every cow and ½d. for every calf weaned. This document is remarkable if only for what it leaves out – there are no sheep mentioned or the fleece they produced, or any of the staple products such as wheat, rye or oats. That apples grew in abundance in the area is born out by the fact that in 1791 William Hillyer is listed as a 'bodkin and apple merchant', and even in the late 19th century cider was made at Heanage Farm in Chobham, and the Sutton family were making cider at Burrow Hill in the early 20th century.

In a court case between Henry Sims and John Harcourt at Guildford Assizes on 30 July 1770, when use of land at Warren Farm in Frimley was in dispute, the crops then growing on this farm were itemised. They included 40 acres of wheat and the same of barley, rye, peas, beans and oats. These appear to have been crops grown for centuries in Surrey Heath. In 1636 Gilbert Neve of Windlesham left at the time of his death 'a chest with a bushel of pease in it'[4] and wheat and rye. Henry Woods in 1603, a Chobham smallholder, left corn, rye, French wheat, peas and barley.

The animals kept were horses, cows, oxen, calves, sheep and pigs. All animals were prized, even mules, and in 1779 Mr Larmer of the *Red Lion* at Blackwater advertised in the *Reading Mercury* 'One of the most handsomest Mules in the

3 *Sheep-shearing at Stanner's*

4 *Turf cutter*

kingdom … any person wanting to purchase so useful and beautiful an animal'[5] could apply to him for more details. The most valued birds commonly kept by the smallholder were geese. There are many examples in the 18th century of geese being stolen, especially in the winter. The geese were kept on the common land, as at Frimley Green where the current village green was known as Goose Garsen Green. The keeping of geese was a long-held tradition and in 1599 Thomas Gonner was required to provide for the lord of the manor 12 pullets at the Feast of St Bartholomew and six geese known as green geese at Pentecost.[6] Turkeys were also kept, and William Elmes, a manorial tenant in 1783, had to make payment of 18 turkeys and 18 groats (each groat was an old 4d.).[7] An occupation that has given us the name of an estate in Frimley today is that of a warrener or keeper of rabbits, and the warren was an important food source. In

1726 George Kershier, a warrener, was granted permission to build a new cottage on waste land in Frimley, and it is most likely this would have been the site of the present estate of that name.[8] There would also have been an abundance of game, but taking it was a risky business as Thomas Blundell, a tailor in Bisley, found in 1669 when he was fined £20 'if he do never hereafter destroy any more game, contrary to Law, that is to say Deare, Pheasants, Partridges, Heathpoults, Ducks Etc'.[9]

PRODUCE AND BENEFITS OF THE HEATHLAND

The commons, waste or heathland that surrounded the farms had a value to those with the traditional right of use, as they could benefit from its produce. Common heaths were owned by the lord of the manor, but those with commonable rights were entitled to use of the land. These rights were known as Turbary, the cutting of turf and peat, and Common of Pasture or Cow-leaze, the right to graze animals. Common in the Soil was the right to extract sand and gravel, but not stone, a commodity considered too valuable. Pannage was the right to turn pigs into the woods to graze on the acorns and mast. Estovers, a Norman-French term, was the right to cut the long heath (top of the heather), gorse, furze, bracken and reeds, as well as wood to the thickness of an arm.

Until other fuels became available with better road transport and the building of the Basingstoke Canal, almost every householder relied on the root of the heather and gorse, usually described in the records as turf or turves, to heat their houses and cook their food. This dependence on a limited supply of fuel kept the population of the area low, with a reasonably constant number of residents and houses until the 19th century. The cutting of turf from the heath was a specialised task requiring careful husbandry of a valuable commodity so that the supply could be maintained. In Surrey Heath, Bisley was the only village without an abundance of turf for its needs. By the mid-18th century villagers were importing their turf from surrounding villages. It is not clear there was ever turf of sufficient quantity in Bisley. Early references to the fuel in the parish records are just for carting turf for the poor. In 1838 there was an agreement which provided them with turf, as a letter from the churchwardens to the new Poor Law Commissioners pointed out:

> For over forty years we have rented part of Chobham Common for the poor of our Parish solely for the purpose of cutting turf for the poor [… It is] no service whatever for the Farmers as they purchase their fireing at Frimley being of better quality and having no waste land in our parish that will produce fireing.[10]

It is known that the turf from Frimley was of good quality as those making pots at Cove and Farnborough also purchased it from the village for their kilns.

It is generally assumed that gorse or furze and broom, which grow so freely on this soil today, are native to the area. There is much evidence to indicate otherwise. In *A complete body of husbandry: collected from the practice and experience of the most considerable farmers in Britain*, Mr Bradley refers to a Mr Fitzherbarde who, in 1500, had written on subjects such as the improvement of heath, furze, gorse and

5 *Bee Skep sketch*

broom ground, which Bradley compared to his own views on the subject.[11] He also detailed the crops grown. There were evidently two types of furze in 1727: the native and that which had been planted, known as French furze. Bradley thought the effort of cutting the small native plant 'is rather more worth than the value of it when cut' although it was good for baking and brewing.[12] The French variety, which grew much larger, was planted for firing. Fitzherbarde said in 1500, presumably before they were planting the French variety, that they were of such value to householders that they 'would not give an acre of gorsy land for two acres of arable'.[13] Bradley went on to explain that in the West Country farmers grew furze on plots, cutting them when six years old and replanting to give them successive crops. The first local reference to the planting of furze seeds is in 1777 when the land around the Pest House (a small building erected to isolate people suffering from infectious disease) at Bagshot was enclosed.[14] The churchwardens at Windlesham made a laurel hedge around this land and purchased 1½ pounds of furze seeds at a cost of 1s. 6d. to sow there.

Of the broom, which Bradley said was sometimes planted as a shelter belt for game, there was again an imported variety, which he said had definite benefits. This was known as Spanish broom, and had an abundance of sweet – smelling flowers so attractive to bees he felt that farmers should grow fields full of it to improve the production of honey and wax. Bees would be kept by the smallholder or his wife, 'especially by cottagers who dwell on the borders of the commons and heaths where the purple-blossomed heath and other odoriferous plants abound'.[15] The traditional skeps used to house the bees at this time were woven from straw and placed on a stool (with holes in the seat to allow access to the interior of the skep) and sited near to the heathland. The number of people keeping bees allowed at least one man, James Lee in Bagshot, to advertise as a beehive maker for a number of years in the late 19th century. Bees were a valuable commodity and like most items with a value, they belonged to the lord of the manor. In the court rolls for Frimley in 1604 it was noted that 'Henry Westend has in his custody a stall of strayed bee, those same bees being pertinent to the Lord of the Manor'.[16] In 1608 the value of four swarms of bees taken by Walter Cooper was 12s. 4d. and in 1609, when Mabel Mersham, a widow, informed them she had 'le Swarme of bees which she has found in a tree', they were valued at 18d. or 1s. 6d. Obviously the value of the bees depended on the number in a swarm.

The marginal farmer in Surrey Heath would have had to make full use of any of the available common rights of the heath and its produce; many of the ideas put forward by Bradley and Fitzherbarde were common practice here. Villagers sent their animals, including cows, to graze on the common accompanied by a child, a practice continued until at least the early 20th century. They also collected bracken for use in animal bedding and for clamping their vegetables. Heather made a simple but effective thatch for small agricultural buildings and for the poorer cottages. Gorse would be used for a lively fire when the housewife was baking, for the base of haystacks to deter rats, or dug into trenches around growing crops to deter moles. A by-product of broom were long pliable withies suitable for basket-making.

6   *Ploughing in Frimley, 1870s*

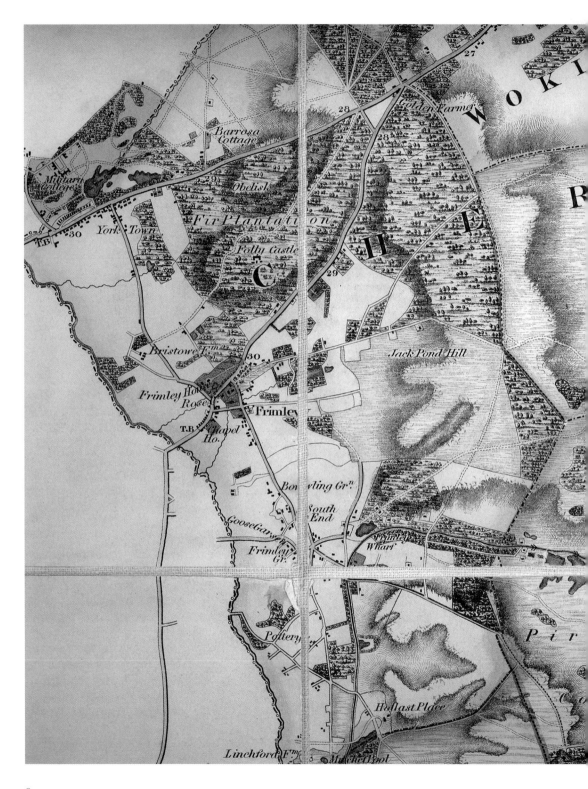

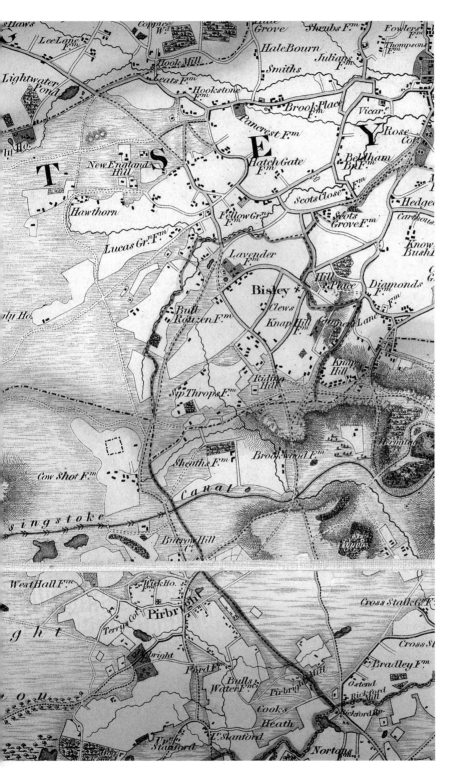

7 *Plantations of pine trees on A. Bryant's map of 1823*

8 *The Boyce family's harvest on Windmill Field*

CHANGE DUE TO ENCLOSURE OF THE HEATHLAND

The Enclosure Act for Frimley in 1801 was the first of the local large-scale enclosures which took place in the 19th century. Windlesham followed Frimley with the enclosure of 4,156 acres in 1812. The Acts relating to Chobham and Bisley were instigated in 1836, although it is not clear when land in Chobham was enclosed, other than 29 acres in 1853 at Chobham Place Woods and the Common Fields at West End, Chobham.[17] With each Act, those who owned freehold or held copyhold property were entitled to a proportion of the newly enclosed land proportionate to that which they already owned. Men like James Lawrell, the lord of the manor of Frimley, who had systematically acquired copyhold property as it fell vacant or purchased it from tenants prior to enclosure, were awarded huge tracts of land. To pay for the cost of the commissioners and surveyors appointed to oversee the introduction of this apportionment, some parcels were sold by auction. In both Frimley and Windlesham 'Poor Allotments' were set aside for those who lost their traditional rights to the land.

Each allotment of land had to be either fenced off or ditches had to be dug around the entire boundary; this was a labour intensive and expensive task, and an example of this type of ditch can still be seen along the Maultway. The ditch or fence, according to a report in 1807, was made by cutting clods from the surface of the outer extremity of the land and piling them as a sloping wall, backed by earth to form the ditch in front. Additional clods were dug from the land until a tolerable fence was made (at a cost of approximately 8d. a yard).[18] The bank was then planted with furze or withy. Around some of the land a temporary fence was provided by a post-and-single-rail fence, which supplied a notion of the boundary of the land until the more permanent boundary was able to consolidate and grow. The report implied that French furze, as mentioned by Bradley, was preferred to the native variety. One paragraph explained that 'In some fields in Frimley, Furze has been sowed after the first green crop, and apparently thrives tolerably well. It is cut for bavins (faggots) for the oven or lime-kiln.'[19] It is of course likely that, with the growth of the brick-making industry in Windlesham and the still-profitable pottery industry in Frimley and Farnborough, the bavins would have been utilised for more than the burning of lime.

There had been a number of theories about how heathland could be used; William Stevenson, in his book *Agriculture of Surrey* published in 1809 described long-held views about the problems of working with this soil and explained how he felt the heathland should be developed, views which in many ways echoed those of Bradley:

> The whole of these extensive heaths may be fairly considered, in their present condition, as of very insignificant value. A very few poor looking cattle and sheep are seen scattered over some of them, picking up a scanty support with much difficulty and labour. Turf is perhaps the produce they afford in the greatest abundance, and of the most value: in the low swampy parts about Bagshot, Windlesham, Frimley and Chobham peat is cut: though as the spots that support it are few, the time it takes to renew is very long, and the demand for it great, it is wearing out fast. Some women in the neighbourhood of Bagshot employ themselves in cutting long heath where it can be got, for besoms, by which they make about 3s a week. Others are employed in gathering the blayberry or whortleberry for sale. Such are the miserable productions and trifling employment which these heaths in general afford. In some of the western heaths however a more profitable mode of occupation has been long followed – one which ought to be withdrawn from more fertile soils, and confined to the wastes. Fish-ponds are common in the western heaths and certainly pay better than any other mode of employing the land; but as their extent must necessarily be confined, there is still room for plantations: and probably, if the hollows were made into fish-ponds and the other part of the heath planted with Scotch fir, or larch, they would yield as much profit as could be expected for them.[20]

In Frimley it is clear that this land was rapidly planted with fir trees. Not long after the heath had been planted the report dated July 1807 found that:

> Much more of it appears to have been planted than otherwise cultivated, chiefly perhaps because from the usual exaggeration of Books and of those persons who are advocates for Planting Timber, it was supposed that little expense was requisite for that kind of prospective improvement. Planted firs therefore occupy above 1000 acres, but many of the plants are dead and very few appear to have made any considerable shoots. I do not see what reason there is to suppose that those which have been carelessly planted will ever arrive at the dignity of Timber.

9 *Sheep in Chobham*

The unnamed writer (initials J.R.) stated that the cause of the stunted growth was the poor soil and that it had a pan of 'rust', or encrusted gravel, which was difficult to penetrate even with a pickaxe. In some areas trees had been planted in furrows, which had produced better results but it was considered extremely laborious for the horses and caused damage to the ploughs. He went on to say that:

> In passing the Golden Farmer Hill to Frimley, more than a mile of the turnpike road is bordered on one side by a belt of Plantation for which the land has been trenched … a mixed plantation; the Larches are tallest, but the Scottish Firs and Silver Firs rather thicker and stouter: on the other [side of the road] by a very extensive plantation where a small hole has been dug for each fir plant, and where of course it has to contend for nutriment with the roots of the surrounding Heath … I scarcely saw a single Fir which had made any shoot; many are dead or have withered.[21]

Improvement of the Land

It was reported that smallholders tried to grow crops on the newly enclosed land. The report of July 1807 stated:

> The surface is always pared with more or less severity and burned into ashes, which are spread on the surface or ploughed in. Green crops are then sowed, till by successively deeper Ploughings and animal manure it can afford to bear corn without ruinous exhaustion, which is irreparable as the surface can be burnt no more. The longer Corn is delayed the better; but as may be supposed in the case of indigent Cultivators the fable of the Goose who was killed for her Golden Egg is too often applicable and from this cause much of the new Inclosure at Frimley lies in a state of hopeless sterility.[22]

More prudent farmers were prepared to sow rye, which was cropped by sheep that fertilised the land with their dung, eventually enabling the farmer to grow root vegetables. Others found that clover was a better crop and that potatoes exhausted the soil less than corn. A few new farms were gradually established on this former heathland at the northern edge of Frimley: Whitehill and Barossa farms were just north of the turnpike road and New Farm approximately where Firwood Drive is today. These were established by 1840 but the majority of those farming the land were extending their marginal arable fields, rather than building new farmhouses surrounded by newly enclosed land. Others, especially in Windlesham, used the land for nursery fields, growing the plants that were brought back from overseas by plant hunters, which thrived in this soil.

There were always theories on how marginal farming land could be improved. James Malcolm gave a list of ways to improve the county's soil: the manures he recommended were made from horse, cow, farmyard and hog dung; night soil, chalk, lime gypsum and marl; bones, woollen rags, horn shavings, tanners bark; furriers clippings and fellmongers cuttings; boiled hops and refuse from breweries; sugar scum; cleaning of ditches and scrapings from roads; mud from ponds and street sweepings; scavengers stuffs and rubbish from old buildings. It seems, in fact, almost anything and everything was used.[23]

Post-Enclosure Farming

The 1801 crop returns for Surrey included wheat, barley and oats, with smaller quantities of potatoes, peas, beans, turnips and rape and rye for Chobham. The same crops were also grown in Bagshot and Windlesham.[24] There were no figures available for Bisley and Frimley. The clergy were requested to make the return at a time when prices were inflated due to the Napoleonic wars. Brayley states that Chobham farmers rotated their crops in a four-year cycle: 'Year 1 Turnips, dunged, hoed twice and folded off; 2 Barley, with one or two ploughings; 3 Clover, dunged or dressed with peat ashes, or both; 4 Wheat; or occasionally 1 Turnips; 2 Oats; 3 Clover; 4 Wheat.'[25] Rye was also sown in August as an early feed in the spring for fattening sheep.

What quality the crops were is not known other than from stray references. Stevenson noted:

> About Chobham and Bagshot the meadow hay has a very fine colour, and to
> all appearances is very excellent hay; but it has been proved by the experience
> of almost every regiment of cavalry ... that it possesses very little nourishment
> ... This curious fact is attributed, and probably with justice ... to the nature
> of the waters at Bagshot ... [being] very strongly impregnated with iron; this
> must injure the hay.[26]

Stevenson also noted that farmers in Bagshot, Windlesham and Chobham
had planted hops as a subsidiary crop. They appear to have been grown over
the centuries as they were paid as tithes in 1595 and were still planted in
Windlesham in 1811. Letters attached to the Enclosure Award refer to a small
crop on land near the *Three Mariners* in Bagshot.[27]

The more prosperous farms with the most fertile land were in Chobham
and Windlesham, where cows and sheep were kept alongside the growing of
crops. Calves were reared for the London market but, according to Brayley,
'this employment has much declined, except in the more retired districts about
Chobham and Bagshot'.[28] He also describes the decline in the number of sheep
kept due to the 'great destruction of these animals by the rot, about the years
1827 and 1828', but they were still to be found in substantial numbers grazing
on Bagshot heath. Brayley's report indicates that farmers were continuing a
tradition, which, in most instances in Surrey was in decline. The numbers of
sheep declined not only as the land was enclosed or used for other purposes,
such as plant nurseries or brick making, but as newer breeds of sheep did not
thrive on heathland.[29] There were still flocks of sheep kept by Bagshot farmers
until at least 1838, when a sale at Hall Grove included '57 Southdown sheep
couples, 25 ewe and wether tegs and a 4 tooth-ram'.[30] Whereas in Chobham,
when John Daborn's farm was sold near Emmetts Mill in 1839, there were
no sheep at all, just cows and calves.[31] Although sheep were perhaps less
common by the early 20th century, local postcards show them being sheared
and driven through Chobham village.

Timber plantations were always a source of income but landholders
did not always get the return they hoped for, although the labour to fell,
cut, and remove it from the site provided valuable employment. In 1894,
40 oaks and 87 elms were felled on Shrubbs Farm which was owned by the
Caldwell family.[32] The cost of cutting and 'drawing out' was just over £18
and the additional cost of the timber merchant's commission was over £16.
Mr Caldwell received £19 for cordwood and £50 for the timber, leaving him
a profit of just over £33 – his comment was that 'the timber was valued at
£148 what a sacrifice!!!' In 1928 men were still employed in woodland work
at Bagshot Park, where Bill Clark and Jimmy Garrett cleared and coppiced
trees and cut hedges.[33] Woodland, or 'cover', also provided additional seasonal
income for some men as beaters for the shooting, which took place in all of
the villages. Lightwater was renowned for its snipe, and the rights were let
annually, providing a further income for the farmer or landowner. In 1890,
the annual return for shooting rights at Uphall Farm in Chobham was £25
and by 1896 it had increased to £45.[34]

WAGES AND CONDITIONS

It was not just adult men who were employed in agriculture; the wives, sons and daughters of farmers and smallholders were also an important source of labour. The income a labourers' wife or child could earn might make all the difference between survival and having to apply for parish relief. The authorities in Victoria's reign became increasingly aware of the numbers of women taking employment rather than staying at home to look after the family, and were equally concerned at the length of time children were absent from school. In a *Royal Commission on the Employment of Children, Young Persons and Women in Agriculture* published in 1867, one local farmer, Frederick Daborn of Chobham, was questioned about the wages he paid and the conditions of employment he offered:

> I pay my carter 15/- a week – he also has 6d. every time he is away and that amounts to about 1/6d. a week. My carter, two under-cowmen and shepherd have to be here three and a half hours each Sunday. No women are employed and boys very little until the age of 11 or 12; they earn 4/- to 5/- a week at that age, that is more than they are worth, but we give it to them in order to retain them on the place.[35]

Tekels Castle estate, developed by Captain Charles Raleigh Knight on what had been marginal farmland and former heathland, was employing large numbers of men by the 1860s. The roll-call of those employed by Knight under his foreman, farmer George Hills, in 1867 was 11, including William Huntingford, a carter at Frimley Park since at least 1851. He was earning what appears to be a standard rate for this job of 15s. a week, George Chappel received 16s., six further labourers earned 13s. and Huntingford's son 3s. Knight also employed two women at the rate of 3s.[36] Fluctuations in rates of pay were probably due to supply, demand and weather-related issues. In one Surrey village quoted in the *Commission on Agricultural Labourers Pay* in 1907, a labourer had received 12s. in 1846, 10s. in 1850, 12s. in 1855 and 15s. in 1865.[37] Less was paid in Hampshire, where average earnings for a labourer in Basingstoke in 1867 were 11s. and only 12s. by 1898/9.

For single women, apart from sewing, taking in washing or becoming a servant, labouring was the most common trade found in the records. Tot and Liz Bachelor became legendary in Windlesham due to all

10 *Tot and Liz Bachelor*

15

11   *Cider-making at Heanage Farm*

the photographs taken of them by Mr Hames of Updown Hill. The sisters were atypical as they never married, retaining their trade as labourers to a considerable age. They lived in Baigents Lane in Windlesham, probably 'living in' when they had a long-term job. According to Allan Jobson:

> At Green Farm lived and worked two sisters, the most queer and distinctive of their kind. They did the work of men, were inseparable and lived much like the cattle they tended … both with full-moon faces, one high-pitched and the other deep and masculine in tone. They tramped about with their skirts tucked up.[38]

Farmers also relied on the supply of itinerant workers who moved around the countryside from season to season. Letters in Thorpe parish records from the vicars of Frimley and Thorpe give an account of one family from Frimley who had become a burden to the poor-rate there. The first letter states that Honour, the wife of Joseph Grainger, had given birth to a child in a field at Thorpe while employed as a pea-picker. The Rev. Stonehouse of Frimley replied that 'there are several families of the Graingers' in Frimley who emigrate about this time of year and live about in barns or otherwise'.[39] Others travelled further; William Collyer of Bisley, travelling with his wife and child, went to Kent in the spring and arrived at the hop-fields at Farnham in the autumn, eventually having recourse to assistance from the Farnham Workhouse.[40] William's wife was suffering from smallpox and the family was transported back to Bisley in an open cart in 1848.

12 *The Benham and Sutton family enjoying a drink of cider*

13 *Ploughing match, Chobham, 4 October 1906*

14 *Mr Benham at the Agricultural Show, Chobham*

SOCIAL LIFE, MARKETS AND FAIRS

As in towns around the country, there were markets held locally for the sale of produce and livestock. There were also ploughing matches, shows and meetings, which brought some colour and social intercourse in what may otherwise have been a dull life. It was very unusual for the markets to be advertised as the dates were set in a social calendar of which everyone would have been aware. However, in 1783 the Knaphill Fair was advertised in the *Reading Mercury* and *Oxford Gazette*, 3 November 1783, alongside another advert for a similar fair nearby at Chobham. One advert stated that the fair would be held as usual at Knaphill, where 'The Fair has been held upwards of 200 years'; the other said that 'by the desire of the gentlemen dealers hereunder mentioned to be held at Chobham … in two commodious fields near the church … to which place we do promise to bring our beast for sale on the 10th day of November 1783 and continue to do so annually'.[41] It is not known if both fairs survived but according to Joy Mason a weekly market in Chobham in 1844 was held in the High Street.[42]

15 *Dairymaids at Medhurst's Farm*

In the *Surrey County Chronicle* in July 1848 there was a report on the prices paid at the Annual Wool Fair held in the yard of the *White Hart* at Chobham. Mr Twycross was the principal purchaser of wool, paying 9d. per pound, but there was no mention of a weekly market. An annual cattle fair at Blackwater, held each November, must have rivalled Knaphill Fair and was still operating up until the 1920s. The fair was a social event as well as a place to sell animals. In 1886, Frederick Street, the Heatherside nurseryman and farmer, visited the fair with his father:

> Monday 8th November – Today we were busy early for it is Blackwater Fair day, both Father and myself went as usual and found a fairly filled fair ... Robert Thicket came by train [from Wonersh] we went all through the cattle and found but few good milch cows ... at last we came across two in calves that would calve in a few days ... So after some continual haggling and bidding between the dealer father bought the 2 for £30 and sent them off by rail to Wonersh. After this we had a search for a pony to drive in the milk cart, and we soon found a very pretty little fellow, which the dealer put into his trap and drove up and down the village in fine style.[43]

The cattle fair at Blackwater was not always such a peaceful place, as Mr Cotterall who was born in Blackwater in 1870 recalled:

> Some of the shows to attend were Mathews from Farnborough and Deakin who lived at Blackwater. A boy was stabbed at the cokernut stall ... the cadets [Royal Military College] used to go to Blackwater Fair which they regarded as fair game, one night they smashed up the Kinema show and had to pay something like £80 in damages.[44]

16   *Agricultural workers at rest, Frimley, 1870s*

It was likely that, for the general sale of animals all year round, farmers would have taken stock to the busier market towns of Guildford, Reading and Basingstoke. The Lammas Fair, held at Chertsey each year in August, which also sold general livestock, had the additional name of 'Black Cherry Fair'. A report in the *Surrey County Chronicle* in 1848 stated that 'black cherries have always been looked for at this fair but, on account of the season, not any were exposed for sale'.[45] Although there was less farming in Surrey Heath by the start of the 20th century, a cattle and general market was still held at Blackwater each week. Reginald Dean, who also held the Kingston and Guildford markets, advertised in the *Camberley News* in 1924 that cattle, pigs, sheep, poultry, eggs and dairy products could be sold there. Guildford was the busiest of the markets and men like Malcolm Bell, who lived in Bisley, were able to make a living as a drover: 'he was one of the original cattle drovers. He would walk and drive cattle from this area to Guildford Cattle Market for 2/- a day.'[46]

Life was not always about work and each year there were local Agricultural Shows. In November 1873 the *Surrey Advertiser* reported that the Chobham,

Windlesham, Horsell and Bisley Agricultural Show was flourishing. It stated that the annual show had started in 1866 and attractions consisted of a root show, held in a marquee erected in the cricket field behind Chobham church, and ploughing matches at High Field and Brick Field which were owned by Mr Fladgate and Mr Daborn. In 1929, the headed notepaper used by the committee of the show stated that the Society was founded in 1851 – no supporting evidence has been found for either of these dates.

Agricultural Unrest

Just over the border in Berkshire there were incidents in 1830 known collectively as the 'Swing Riots', where arson and machine-breaking took place, fuelled by the introduction of new machinery and low pay. Despite alternative work being available in the nurseries in Surrey Heath, a few incidents of unrest still occurred. In April 1840 John Mears, the Bagshot solicitor, received a letter from Sir Edmund Currey of Erlwood:

> You will have heard of the fire that occurred on the Rapley property on Thursday night – between five and six acres of inferior Scots fir are destroyed – it was lighted near the Poors allotment – I am puzzled as much as ever to think what can be the object of the Incendiary beyond shere wickedness – 20 or 30 of the poor Heath cutters bundles were consumed in the fire – and many more but narrowly escaped the flame.[47]

It was not the first incident of its kind in the area. In May 1839 a meeting had been called in Windlesham where residents resolved that action needed to be taken to protect life and property, as several fires had been started in the area.

17 *Beets and mangolds, West End*

No loss of life had occurred, but people wished to find those 'wretches already guilty of the diabolical acts, in burning the poor man out of his cottage and in the indiscriminate destructions of Plantations and Property'.[48] Further incidents took place in 1848-9 whereby particular men seem to have been targeted in Chobham. In a poster published by Medhurst on 4 January 1849 an award of £100 was offered for information leading to the arrest of the culprits who had set fires on 27 December and 1 January. James Stevens and William Smith eventually pleaded guilty to seven arson attacks. One attack targeted Richard Gude, a rather harsh Guardian of the Poor who lived at Valley Wood. Stevens admitted he 'got a truss of straw and shook it up light. Smith went out to watch while I lighted it. We then ran home'.[49] The next incident was at Mr Collyer's, followed by James Hull's, Mr Hodd's and Lord Vaux's at Highams where:

> It was a cow stall at the end of a barn ... I struck the match and put it in to one of the holes, and then run away over one of Lord Vaux's fields into the Park ... towards the gate. We could not get out the gate, but went 15yds lower down and jumped over into the road. I was then shot at as described by Lord Vaux.[50]

None of the attacks appear to be coordinated with other people or groups, rather, individuals who were tempted into attacking local landowners, perhaps due to high spirits, contempt of the establishment or even lack of employment.

People still farm in Surrey Heath today, but many of the fields are now used for keeping horses, and although cows still graze in the meadows, there are no longer sheep in Bagshot. There are however a few legacies to this aspect of our past life including the annual agriculture and horticulture shows held in West End and Chobham, occasional ploughing matches and the Strawberry Fair in Bisley.

Chapter Two

SUPPLEMENTARY TRADES AND INCOME

As income from farming was often marginal, a number of supplementary trades were carried out by residents of Surrey Heath, the earliest of these being the spinning and weaving of wool and linen in Bisley, Chobham and Windlesham and the making of pots in Frimley and Mytchett.

CLOTH TRADES

In the earliest records the most common secondary industry to supplement the produce and income from the land was weaving or trades associated with clothwork, including shearmen, who trimmed the cloth, and tailors. The vast majority of men worked with wool, occasionally flax or, surprisingly, silk. Weaving was a common trade for smallholders during the 16th and 17th century.

Three men were apprehended in Surrey Heath for burglary in the late 16th and early 17th centuries: John Skynner of Chobham in 1587, William Thompson of Bagshot in 1598 and Arthur Gobye in Bagshot in 1609, each gave their occupation as silk-weavers long before the Spitalfields silk industry was established.[1] A survey in Southwark in 1583 identified workers in the silk trade as including 13 from Holland, one Burgundian and one Frenchman – clearly a trade limited to men from overseas.[2] The reason why men, who appear to have English names and be living in local villages, would have been employed in the exotic silk industry is not clear. The nearest town associated with the silk trade was Reading where weaving was carried out after the Civil War, replacing the earlier cloth trade.

There were a large number of people in Bisley and Chobham, and to a lesser extent in Windlesham, who made cloth for extra money, for many it was their only trade, but none have been identified in Frimley. No wool spinners are identified either, but as this was an occupation usually carried out by women it would have been less likely to occur in records at this time. However, evidence that spinning occurred can be found in an inventory attached to George Martyn's will in 1629.[3] George was a husbandman or small farmer in Chobham, but among his possessions were one woollen wheel and two linen wheels.

Only one dwelling exists today, with evidence that weaving actually took place. Heathcote Cottage is a small timber-framed dwelling on the edge of Bisley

18 *Wool sacks being carted through Chobham*

Common. It would always have made a marginal living, but there is evidence that the upper floors of Heathcote Cottage were used for weaving, as there is a groove in the wooden floor made by the constant pressure of the weaver's heel.[4]

The earliest weavers were named in court records, wills and the 1660s Hearth Tax returns. Too many weavers existed to identify them all, indicating that the trade was commonplace. At Bisley, the Cobbett family appear most often in the records; at Chobham, William Grove, Joseph Luff and Thomas Woods were all identified as weavers in 1661. At Windlesham, no weavers are identified in the Hearth Tax Returns.

Spinning and weaving appear to be an occupation given to residents of village workhouses, as an inventory of goods in Frimley workhouse in 1793 contained '2 Wool baskets … A frame or parts of a Loom … A Spinning Wheel', and in the garret 'a Wool Basket, five Spinning Wheels and two paire of Cardes'.[5] Between the kitchen and workshop there was also another loom frame. Spinning and weaving as an occupation had generally died out locally during the early to mid-18th century but William Pigg in 1740, Thomas Turner in 1803 and his son Joseph in 1811 were still occupied in this trade in Chobham, and in 1762, Thomas Baines was recorded as a weaver in Windlesham.

Some of the field names in the area indicate that flax and woad, used to dye the cloth blue, were grown in Surrey Heath. The fields near the Blackwater River, now part of Yorktown industrial estate, were named Watchett, derived from 'woad sceat', a corner of land where woad grew.[6] Flex lands were fields in Chobham and Frimley. It was not only in ancient times that flax was grown in Frimley Green as 'Old people in the village still remember when the slopes from the windmill to the canal were not scrubland as now, but sheets of blue from the flowers of flax which used to be cultivated there.'[7] In Bisley in 1583 William Rickson was a linen weaver,[8] and in 1700 Thomas Taylor, also of Bisley, was a flax dresser.[9] Flax, according to Stevenson in 1809, was best grown on poor land as it grew too strongly in good soil. According to his report it was not widely grown in Surrey but as it was suitable as a crop for land 'lately broken up', it probably made a good first crop on land garnered from the heath. As he said, 'It is found to be a very good preparation for wheat on thin soils ... it is ripe very early in the summer [and] it can be sold to help pay for the expense of the corn harvest.'[10]

Five tailors worked with the finished cloth at Chobham in the 1660s: George Wheatley, John Pivison, William Tomson, William Grove and George Bullen.[11] This appears far too many for the local population, therefore, a small cottage industry may have existed in the area with goods being sold in Guildford. The close proximity of Guildford, a centre for the production of woollen cloth, provided a market for raw material, woven cloth or their finished goods. At least one man who lived in Chobham could have purchased locally and sent their goods to London for sale. In 1666, possibly to escape the pestilence in London, Robert Wye took over his mother's residence 'Polores or Brockesbourne' on the corner of Chertsey Road, a property later occupied by Edward Burrows the builder.[12] In the document outlining his arrival, Wye is named as a Woollen Merchant of London. Robert may well have been one of only a few men trading at this date, as the *Victoria County History* noted that by 1630 the trade was already in decline. A petition was forwarded to the Privy Council, which threw light on the state of the trade at that time. The petitioners were:

> Clothiers who for many years previously until now of late maintained 1,400 poor people at least in spinning of wools, weaving, working, making, dyeing and fulling and dressing of cloth called Hampshire kerseys. For many years they had sold these kerseys to one Samuel Vassall, a merchant who vented them beyond the seas.[13]

Vassall was now in duress and no other merchant was taking up the trade. Three of the men who signed the petition, Robert, Henry and Timothy Chitty had local names, although in 1630 they were residents of Godalming. William Ellis, a J.P. writing at the time, said that probably 3,000 people were in distressed circumstances, being unable to sell their cloth.

POTTERS

The importance of the local border ware pottery industry, and the role that Frimley and its potters had within that trade, is still far from clear. What is certain is that the basic raw materials, a limited supply of clay and an abundance of good-quality turf for firing were available to men with an aptitude for making pots. The name 'border ware' has been given to pottery produced in north-east Hampshire and north-west

19 *Border ware pottery, all are pipkins or small saucepans – the yellow glaze was made by adding lead*

Surrey, predominantly in Farnborough, Cove, Yateley, Frimley, Mytchett and Ash. The output was primarily plain utilitarian pots and bowls for domestic use. Jacqueline Pearce, in her book *Border Ware, Post-Mediaeval Pottery in London 1500-1700*, maps out the local potteries and gives a history of the trade from the coarser pots to the later products, including the 15th-century 'Tudor Green' bowls which were washed in a pale green glaze before firing. The bulk of the products made would have been for local use, although it is known that some were transported to larger towns. Examples of the type found in London date mainly from the 17th century, when it was distinctive for its yellow and green glazes; the early pots are made from pale grey/cream clay. In the 19th century the potteries in Frimley and Mytchett produced pots, tiles and household wares that were made with red/brown clay.

Early pottery sites are unidentified, but there are field names in Frimley which indicate where kilns were situated.[14] It is believed that one of the potteries was in Burrow Hill, as fields in this location were known as kiln fields. The earliest site known as a pottery was Potshop Field (Potteries Lane) in Mytchett, described in 1790 as 'about 3 acres of land with a messuage or potshop abutting the common on the south and east'.[15] There was a second kiln at Deeks Lane in Frimley Green. The *Miners Arms* and Minehurst Farm are possible names associated with this trade, although given their respective dates their names could also refer to the miners who dug the rail cutting under the Basingstoke Canal in 1838.

While evidence indicates that numerous potters were working near Frimley village, there are no obvious remains of clay pits found nearby, however, Alphington pond may formerly have been one. Potters Pool on the edge of the Basingstoke Canal was formed by the removal of clay to make pots. At Frimley Green it is likely that clay was dug from land which became Wharfenden Lake. The lake was enlarged at the same time the Basingstoke Canal was built, as P.A.L. Vine remarked in his book *London's Lost Route to Basingstoke*. Vine stated that Wharfenden, Mytchett Lake and Great Bottom Flash were not water-filled prior to the canal being built; 'The fact that none of these is marked on any of the original plans suggests they were natural hollows created into reservoirs when the canal was built.'[16] Rather than natural hollows it is probable that they were spent clay and/or stone and gravel pits; some clay having been required to line the canal.

Frimley is the only village in Surrey Heath where potters are known to have worked, other than Chobham's Richard Edmeade in the early 17th century. In

1629 and 1635 John Cantrill was named in the Frimley Court Barons as a potter. In 1637 Robert Gonner, a potter, left his goods and chattels to his family, itemising the tools of his trade. They were 'the pott kill and potting wheel, with the boords belonging … in the ware house potts burnt and greene … the clay without doores'.[17] He was also a smallholder who had 20 sheep, nine lambs and 1½ acres of rye growing. His relative John Gunner held 12 acres of land, known as Sturt land, in the vicinity of Sturt Road today, which in 1635 he leased to Richard Walton, a potter from Farnborough.

20 *17th-century border ware porringer, found by David Howcroft in the eaves of Cumber Cottage in Ford Road, Bisley in 1970, just prior to the demolition of the cottage*

It appears there was a movement of potters back and forth across the border, with a number of intermarriages between the families. The Rogers, alias Marner, family had, from the 16th century, been able to dig for the white clay at Farnham Park.[18] In 1648 when John Rogers, alias Marner, died, he was a potter in Farnborough, and in 1719 Herman Rogers and his wife Katherine moved to Frimley.[19] Herman probably acquired his Germanic Christian name from Harmon Reynolds, another of the Farnborough potters.

The Mason family was another to arrive in Frimley in the early 18th century. In 1720 Richard Mason of Cove appeared in Frimley court records, taking on land. In 1743 he surrendered a house and two acres of land known as Mitchridden to Mary Leigh, whose family had Mytchett Place built the following century. Another branch of the same family, John Mason of Yateley, a potter, married Elizabeth Elmes of Frimley in 1731, and this family was making pots in Frimley until the 19th century. In 1821 George Mason was a potter in Frimley, and when Robert Mason, the son of Robert, was married in the village in 1860, both father and son were still in the trade. The overlap with potters in Yateley includes land near Frimley Chapel where Thomas and William Thrift surrendered their copyhold

21 *Red ware pottery: this was in common use until the early 20th century. It is likely these would have been the type of items produced at Mytchett and Frimley Green*

property known as Church Gate Cottage and one acre of land to Thomas Bristoe of Yateley, who was also a potter.

The last family of potters to arrive in Frimley were the Smiths, who had their main pottery in Farnborough. In 1842 John Smith and his wife Mary were at the pottery in Mytchett, with their son Charles living in a cottage near Mytchett bridge on the canal, almost opposite Potters Pool.[20] John and Mary's eldest son was living in Wharf Road, Frimley Green, with his wife Bufoy, just a short walk from the Guildford Road pottery, and their third son Stephen was living on the Grove at Frimley. George Siggery was also a potter, living in Cross Cottages, the Hatches, in Frimley Green. Siggery could have made the short walk from his home, through the Hatches to Farnborough or to Guildford Road, Frimley Green or Mytchett. In the 1871 Census the potters working in Mytchett were John Smith, who had taken over his father's business, and Robert Siggery, the son of George. At the same time John's son, also named John, ran the pottery at Frimley Green with George Hersey. By 1881 John Smith senior employed just two boys, and by the 1890s, both potteries had ceased trading. In Mytchett in 1891 Bufoy Smith, the widow of John, was living next to the disused kiln and by 1896 she was renting a room to St Andrew's Church as a Sunday School for local children.[21] This area later became a chicken-farm run by Marjorie Foster, the first lady to win the coveted Kings Prize at Bisley for shooting in 1930, and her partner Miss Badcock.

Chapter Three

Workers on the Heathland

Many families and individuals did not live in the centre of the villages but on the heathland, either from necessity or choice. Gypsy families travelled around the area, moving usually on a route decided by the availability of seasonal work or local trade. The families would settle down for a few days or weeks, erect a bender (a temporary shelter made from rods of supple wood and fabric) for daily use and then move on. Single men who lived in rough shelters on the land were known to the villagers and were occasionally employed on the farms, or later on nursery land. Some families earned their living from the natural products of the heathland and erected their homes nearby, there were also those who were forced, through poverty, to make their homes here. The make-up of these settlements varied according to each village. No records exist of early settlements, so it is difficult to say how ancient a tradition it was to settle on the heath. The only written account locally is the *Family of Love* at Bagshot, a 17th-century pseudo-religious group which scandalised local society.

Change brought about by Enclosure

From the beginning of the 19th century with the Enclosure Acts there were family groups at Bagshot, Frimley and Chobham on formerly open heathland. The lord of the manor of Chobham had given half-acre plots of land to poor villagers at Clearmount, north of Burrow Hill, and New England, West End, in 1815; this was to enable them to build homes surrounded by land for growing crops. In Frimley and Windlesham, where land had been set aside under the Acts of Enclosure to make up for the commonable 'rights' being extinguished, a number of men built makeshift cottages.

On the Windlesham fuel allotments, just north of Jenkins Hill, a small colony of men and their families erected basic dwellings near a fresh water spring. An article published in the *Morning Leader* in August 1910 illustrated how one family, William Cole and his wife and children, came to build their home. It is a tale of a family who moved around to find work, unable to rent accommodation as they had five young children at the time, and desperate for a home to call their own. William was the son of Michael Cole, a broom

22 *Gypsies in the snow at Valley End*

maker, and Mary, the daughter of Richard Excell, a brick maker. Although they were married in Warfield parish church in June 1852, four of their five eldest children were baptised at Windlesham.[1] The family arrived back in the village at the Poors Allotment in Bagshot in 1864, but it is not clear where they had been living prior to this; perhaps they had always been moving around the area. However, according to their father they had 'wandered about until they came to the common. There under a tent which they had often used for camping by the roadside on their journeys, they slept for a week or so.'[2] Over a period of 16 months, the Cole family then built themselves a two-roomed dwelling from wood, stone, brick and heather thatch. The stone they collected from a pit near the cottage was arranged as the base for the chimney, and the only purchase made was of a few bricks for the top of the stack. For the cottage, the Cole family paid 5s. rent a year to the Windlesham fuel allotment committee. In 1910, only William and his wife were left and although he was aged 82 'he still works in the garden and occasionally makes a broom'.[3] The family were eventually moved to Park View Cottages in Bagshot, and despite the harsh conditions in which they had brought up their eight children, Mary died in 1918 aged 87 of influenza and William in 1920 aged 92 from senile decay. Few families of this status have been interviewed about their lives, and the Cole's is perhaps fairly typical of the struggle to find a site for a home, which the setting up of the poor allotments alleviated, although it is not what they were primarily intended for. Of the remaining occupants of the dwellings erected at Bagshot, just off the Guildford Road in Frimley Green and in Chobham Road at Frimley, all the men were labourers, broomdashers or chimney sweeps.

23   *Collection of cottages, Windlesham Fuel Allotment*

It was not just the poor allotments that housed people. In 1841 at Wishmoor Cross, an area of heathland in Frimley close to the Windlesham fuel allotments, was a settlement which became known as the Hermitage.[4] Two labourers, James Hoptroff and James Estridge lived at the Hermitage, with their families totalling 12 people, at a site some distance from the main road. At Frimley on The Grove and along the Portsmouth Road were a number of hastily-erected dwellings which were cleared by 1871 and large new mansions were erected in their stead. Although enclosure caused much change in the way of life for villagers and reduced their long-held rights, there were opportunities for some to establish a family home on land which, until this time, had been wholly administered by the lord of the manor.

TRAVELLERS AND GYPSIES

It is probable that gypsy families had been travelling around the heathland for generations, so it is difficult to establish how many there were or when they arrived. None are identified as gypsies in burial records in Surrey Heath until the late 19th century, and there are no payments to the families from any of our parishes for relief. It could be that many of those buried as 'strangers' or 'unknown' in parish registers were from the travelling families, but as so many people 'tramped' to find work it is difficult to make this assumption. True gypsies were Romany, a wandering race originating in north-west India, but by the 19th century there were also 'tinkers', generally from Ireland. Census returns give the best idea of the areas in which the Gypsies travelled. In the 1881 Census, five local groups of Gypsies lived at the Folly in West End, and all were listed by the official

24 *Gypsies with a bender*

enumerator as having 'No occupation – Gypsies'.[5] Of the five families, Henry Green was born in Binstead; James and Mary Ann Lamb were from Farnham and Guildford; George Lamb and his four children were enumerated without any birthplace; Aaron Green was born at Chertsey and their five children were born at Longcross, Ascot, Warfield, Chobham and the Folly, West End. The fifth family was Alfred and Alice Gregory, Alfred was from Cookham in Berkshire and his wife from Thornby in Gloucestershire. Their six children were born at Farnham, Gloucester, Wokingham, near Maidenhead and the Folly, West End. The youngest

25 *Gypsies under bender*

26 *London Mothers' Convalescent Home*

two children, Aaron Green junior and Ellen Gregory, were aged two months and one year respectively, which implies they stayed longer in the area than just a few days. This could be due to the work of Stanley Alder, a teacher at the Shaftesbury School in Bisley, who wrote about his involvement with the family from 1881-91.[6] The families were gradually encouraged to leave their travelling way of life and take a cottage in the village; the first of these families was James Baker, already earning his living as a chimney-sweep by 1881, and his wife who, according to Stanley Alder, made beehives. They had five children with them by 1891: James, 17; George, 12; Walter, six; Ernest, three; and Sophia, aged one. The Baker family moved into a cottage in Lucas Green, West End, near to Frees Farm where the farmer Thomas Harrison allowed them to congregate on the farm for meetings. Harrison's farm was a place where the families knew they could gain shelter, and probably find work, as several gypsies were noted in the 1891 Census as having slept in their barn overnight, leaving before 6am the following day. Eight families, 10 males and 15 females, were sleeping in tents near Frees Farm at the time of the Census.[7]

Gypsy families were employed seasonally on farms and nurseries, but the numbers in the area increased dramatically when there was any kind of occasion relating to races, fairs or military manoeuvres. The families would attend the Ascot race-meetings, setting out stalls or fairgrounds, running sideshows or selling their hand-made goods or their ponies. In addition to families in West End there were three fair carts in Chertsey Road, Windlesham in 1881, and these travelling fairground people would set up their attractions at the annual round of traditional village events, including markets and agricultural shows. According to a Constabulary Force Committee report in the *Reading Mercury* in 1839, some groups of gypsies would also play their fiddles in local public houses.[8]

27   *Whittle's Fair*

Anyone who has lived in the area for a long time can recall the gypsy camps and their visits each year:

> The gypsies used to come from all over England to Chobham Common and there used to be an encampment by the Monument during Royal Ascot Week. They used to come with their horse-drawn vehicles and all the horses were out on the common ... I can see them now walking past my Mum's house with the heather they had gathered on the Common and they used to take it up to Royal Ascot and sell it on the street – lucky heather. There is still white heather on the common.[9]

One or two families gave their occupation in 1891 as 'Gypsy Hawker': an indication that the pegs and other items, which they made from hedgerow plants, would be sold at doorsteps and fairs. Charles Baker was the only one who gave his occupation as a peg-maker in 1881 and above this description were the words 'wood turner', a possible reference to the wooden dahlias they made. In 1891, Baker was still earning his living as a peg-maker and his wife was a hawker. Gypsies were known for making birch brooms rather than heather brooms and would also collect moss from the common and sell it to nurserymen. The families kept chickens, as well as donkeys or horses for hauling their carts, and one man in Bisley remembered the site of their caravans moving from the village with a basket of hens straddled over the axle of the undercarriage.[10] Gypsy families are still known, even today, to collect heather to sell on the streets of Camberley.

34

Gypsies were generally accepted in the community, but as soon as large houses were built near to the edge of the common and on former heathland there was conflict between these new residents and gypsies with regard to their traditional camping sites. Letters to Lord Onslow's agent from J. Barring White of Parker's Hill in Chobham are typical of the attitude of the new community to the travellers; he wrote in 1919 that he wished to have someone appointed to remove this 'perfect pest'. There are probably six or seven lots of them on the Common and all the residents are complaining, and Mr Roberts of the Ridgemount Estate, the Golf Club and others are exasperated'.[11] J. Barring White's view was echoed in a letter from Miss Hay-Drummond, who was one of the ladies who ran the London Mothers' Convalescent Home, which stood near the railway bridge at Broomhall. She was concerned that gypsies were upsetting the mothers sent there for recuperative care, as they were camped opposite the home and were 'very dirty, also begging'. One common concern, revealed by Mr Barring White, was that, 'the presence of these gypsies on the Common is undoubtedly depreciating the [value of] property in this neighbourhood'.

The golf course provided employment for at least one young Romany girl, Bathsheba Smith, as she recalled 'I worked when I was 11 years old over against the golf course (Sunningdale) I carried they clubs for you sometimes two lots, they were heavy and I only got 1/6d. I knows what all they clubs is called'.[12] As more housing estates were built, new golf courses established and more people moved out from towns to the countryside, the conflict between gypsies and residents became greater. Increased pressure was placed on travellers to give up their traditional lifestyle, a problem which is still pertinent today.

28 *Interior and exterior views of local van*

HAWKERS AND CHAPMEN

As early as the 1851 Census it seems likely that many people who were occupying small cottages on the heathland were only one step away from a travelling life. Elizabeth Parker of Mytchett was enumerated as a 76-year-old hawker, who stated her place of birth as 'unknown'. She was surrounded by an extended family who all gave occupations that were similar to those of travellers, including a cutler, grinder and brazier, and a mat and mop maker. Making and selling mats supported more than one family in Surrey Heath. Living at the Folly in West End in 1891 was William Penfold, who was a hawker selling brushes and mats. Hawkers and chapmen required little education, and many of the products required would have been collected as scrap or available free from the heathland. If the mats and mops were made from old woollen rags, as the poorest were at this time, it is likely the flailed stems of the gorse would have been used as a woven backing, and saplings grown on the heath utilised as mop handles. It could also be supposed that the heat required by a cutler to repair knives, scissors and razors would require a brazier fuelled by gorse as it provided the fiercest heat.

Hawkers and chapmen generally made their living by selling in the street or at the back doors of cottages; they were usually unwelcome at larger houses. Among those listed as hawkers in 1851 were James Cheeseman of Chertsey Road in Windlesham, Isaac Smith in Bagshot, and Moses White and Frances Williams at Mudd Town (Camberley today). Eventually, the number of people taking up this way of life was considered a nuisance and hawkers had to be registered and carry passes. In Bagshot there was a man known as 'Sailor Jack', who resided at a common-lodging house who made a living from selling matches and running errands for people. In the *Reading Mercury* in December 1859 it was reported that he had been set upon by some ruffians who had stolen the 14s. he was carrying on behalf of members of a local society, and had injured him so badly he was bed-ridden for some time.[13]

Costermongers, who sold fruit and vegetables from their handcarts, named after the 'costers', a type of apple sold, also traded, as well as fish sellers who sold their goods from horse-drawn carts, and pie-and-muffin men. Traders who operated without having a retail outlet in the form of a shop, were usually considered to be hawkers, as were those who entertained local people with their musical organs and dancing bears as they passed through the villages. In the 1920s and '30s local people were, once again, reduced to a hawker's way of life when there was mass unemployment. Percy Elkins, who was born at Broomhall in 1906, was one local man whose license to trade is now held at Surrey Heath Museum.

BROOMDASHERS

Broomdashers were men who made brooms from the product of the heath: the long heather for the head and occasionally saplings for the handle. Brooms were traditionally made in at least two sizes: the broom or besom for sweeping the floor, and a small hand-held version for hearths and ledges.

Although considered to be an ancient trade in Surrey Heath, the first reference found to broomdashers was the purchase of staves or broom-handles for Thomas Elks by the Overseers of the Poor in Windlesham in 1726. It is likely Elks was

30 *Organ Grinders*

31 *Village fishmonger at Chobham*

infirm, as there are also payments which included 'bleeding him'. Thomas died in February 1732/3.[14] It was stated in 1801 that at Windlesham 'Some of the poor pull heath for the purpose of making Brooms – a Manufactory of that sort being carried on at the Workhouse.'[15] It is likely that, prior to the 19th century, broom dashing was work given to feeble or elderly men or women. It could have been another secondary trade, perhaps taking over after the decline of weaving, when it would have provided additional income for a subsistence holding. One earlier note exists in the Bisley registers in 1709 to Thomas Taylor, 'a brooman', and John and Jethro Cheeseman appear in the Quarter Session records in 1770 as broom makers from Bisley, as did Samuel Cheeseman in 1819.[16] Broom dashing appears to have finished as a trade in Bisley by the early 19th century, even though by the mid-19th century it was a very productive time in Frimley and Bagshot. No references exist in the Chobham records to the trade, even though it is known there were men employed making brooms at West End by 1851.

It is clear the trade of broom dashing was associated with the poor. In the *Reading Mercury* and *Oxford Gazette* in December 1784, it was reported that a couple employed in the broom trade were found dead on heathland at Aldershot. Mr and Mrs Harrington were aged 60 and 70 and had brought up a family of 18 children. They had walked to Overton to visit one of their daughters and walked back to their home in very cold weather, 'the poor woman was found lying on her side, dead, with her husbands stick and a bundle by her; and about 200 yards distance, the husband was found.' The Coroner's verdict was that they had 'Died through extreme fatigue, abstinence from proper nourishment and the inclemency of the weather.'[17]

According to Gertrude Jekyll in *Old West Surrey*, 'Among the broom-squarers or broom-squires there have always been some very rough characters … But there are many good, honest hard-working men'.[18] Jekyll went on to describe broom dashing as a cottage industry where the materials cost the makers very little, and where in 1904 a dozen of the heath brooms could be purchased for 2s. 6d. and those from birch for 3s. 6d.

In 1841, more men were identified in the Census as broom makers than in 1851, perhaps because men like William Cole were enumerated as agricultural labourers, or it could be the result of some of the landowners removing men from land required for building large houses. Some broom makers lived in hastily erected post-enclosure dwellings, some little more than shelters, near to land with an abundance of heather. Gertrude Jekyll described the shelters used by the broom makers as a shed thatched with heather.[19] An example would be three cottages erected on the Portsmouth Road, where Southcote Park is today, which were occupied in 1841 by David North, Charles North and Thomas Moth and their young families. By 1871, after the heather was exhausted, the broom maker's cottages were demolished to make way for homes for the gentry.

For local broom makers, the trend seemed to have moved away from using heather in the late 19th century, and brooms were constructed from more standard materials such as birch. In 1891 men were still producing heather brooms in Bagshot. In the *Post Office Directory* in 1862 and 1867, Henry Draper of Bagshot was listed as a 'Bass Broom Maker' and from 1878 Thomas Hockley described himself in local directories as a 'Broom Merchant' in Bagshot, making birch brooms. Edward Hockley was still making birch brooms until 1907. The making of the brooms varied with the materials used, according to Gertrude Jekyll, the birch having to be cut and dried so that it became tougher before it was used. Two bonds of hazel or withy were used to tie heather to the handle of a broom, and three were used for birch. The bonds could not be made of dry material, so the wood was soaked in a pond or pool of water until it was pliable.[20]

Bass brooms were probably made along with heather brooms as there was still a local trade for these. William Cole and probably others were making brooms for sale well in to the 20th century, although none were listed in any 20th-century trade directories. It is not known if middle-men sold these goods on to shops or if they were sent to larger towns for sale by the individual broom makers. It is also

32 *1726 Parish Account: Windlesham broom staves*

33   *Home of William and Mary Cole*

unclear when the production of heather brooms finished, although it is known that local shops offered them for sale until at least the outbreak of the Second World War. The passing of the broom trade saw the end of way of life which had provided an income for many families; the raw materials cost them nothing but hard labour, and grew in abundance on our heathland.

BRICK MAKERS

The earliest brick makers worked on heathland between Windlesham and Chobham, extracting the brick earth to make tiles and bricks, with clay suitable for making bricks occuring naturally in this part of the borough. The earliest bricks would have been hand-formed for local use. Brick making was a trade carried on in any area where there were suitable materials; the clay and the fuel for firing the kilns. According to Joy Mason, clay suitable for brick making was found at Brick Hill between Windlesham and Chobham in the late 16th or early 17th century.[21] The earliest brick maker known to have been operating in Surrey Heath was Robert Bishop of Chobham, who was described in 1683 as a brick and tile maker who had lived in the village since at least 1677, when his son John was baptised there.[22]

All the early agreements for extracting brick earth relate to land in the vicinity of Brick Hill. A grant was required from the lord of the manor for the right to extract clay, and the grant was given in exchange for money from the brick

34 *'Broomdashers' Cottage*

35 *Broomdasher display in Surrey Heath Museum*

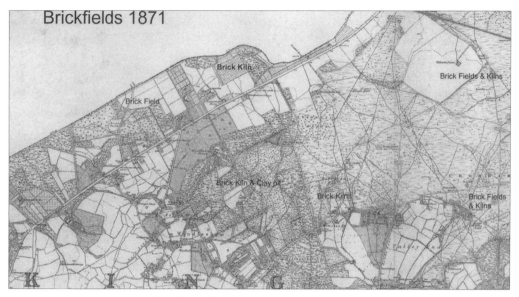

36   *Map of brickfields in Windlesham and Chobham, based on O.S. map 1871*

maker. Grants were awarded on both sides of the Brick Hill area, as it was on the border of two manors. In 1739 Abel Walter, then lord of the manor of Bagshot, leased part of the East Common at Windlesham, near Brick Hill, to the brick maker Thomas Finch, permitting him to dig for brick and tile earth and in 1785 there were still brick and tile kilns on this site.[23] The earliest record of a grant of land given for brick making, according to the Chobham records, was one in December 1751 when Robert Stevens leased half an acre of land at Valley Wood. It appears, from numerous disputes between the brick makers and the commoners, that there were issues arising from grants of land, however, it appears not to have been of great concern when brick making was a relatively small trade for local consumption.

With the enclosure of the land in Windlesham in the early 19th century, brickmakers from other areas arrived and more kilns were built. What had been a local trade employing a small number of men restricted to one area of the borough was now an industry spread over several sites. New kilns were built at Westwood Road and Ribsden in Windlesham, at Broomhall near Sunningdale and on Chobham Common, between Sunningdale and Brick Hill. There was also a later development in the 19th century at Chobham Park Lane. Some of the villagers were quite pleased as the new kilns provided them with work, but others were more concerned with the impact of the industry on the area. Villager's concerns covered issues as diverse as the holes left from the extraction of the clay, which were a danger to people, animals and conveyances, and the huge amount of turf and gorse used to fire the kilns. The residents of Windlesham first raised concerns at the time of the Enclosure Act (see Appendix 1) and they were the subject of a court case in 1873 between the villagers and Robert Lawrence, a brick maker (see Appendix 2 and 3).

The five acres of land which had been granted to Robert Stevens in 1751 was eventually conveyed to Robert Lawrence in 1860; he may have also taken on Thomas Finch's site. The Earl of Onslow also leased him a further 10-acre parcel of Chobham Common with new brick kilns at £50 a year for eight years, when he is described as Mr Robert Lawrence of Waltham St Lawrence, Berks.[24] It is said Mr Lawrence was related to a larger company at Binfield near Bracknell, where by the 1890s Thomas Lawrence and Sons were supplying up to 12 million bricks a year. Lawrence, like all brick makers, was required to restore exhausted land by grassing it over in a 'husbandlike' manner after he had extracted the clay. Before the land grant was conveyed to Lawrence in 1860, the site appears to have been badly run; the land was not fenced off, and a trench cut across the site on the line of an old watercourse to carry excess water was a danger to grazing animals and people crossing the heath.

Of those who worked in the brick making trade, there is little more than their names left in local records to remind us that these men were once important providers of the weekly income. Men employed in the trade in the 19th century carried names from almost every family in Chobham and Windlesham, and at least one family is commemorated today. The Gunner family who had the kilns at Ribsden and built their home opposite is remembered in the house of that name in Chertsey Road.

37 *Bricks and tiles made in Chobham, 1930s*

38   *Brickfields at Brick Hill, Valley End; Medhurst card*

Brick making was a risky trade and there are at least two examples of bankruptcies in the locality. In 1839 the *Reading Chronicle* reported that Frederick and George Prince, brick makers of Sunningwells near Sunningdale, were bankrupt.[25] In 1886 Frederick Street of Heatherside recorded in his diary on 29 September:

> This morning father had to go over to Bracknell to inspect the Bracknell Brick Company's works and stock they having turned bankrupts and The Capital and Counties Banking Co of whom Sir Gabriel is a director is a large creditor and consequently he and they fear where there is value for their money. The bankrupts are to have a sale on the 5th Octbr.[26]

Of the late 19th- and early 20th-century brick making sites, the largest was opened in 1897 by Mr Noble. Known as Parker's Hill Brick Works, the site was opposite the Runic Cross between Chobham and Sunningdale and was owned by John Henry Sturt and his brother-in-law Henry Taylor by 1902. John Sturt had been a brick maker since at least 1883, having sites near the Runic Cross and close to Brick Hill, near a bridge which today carries the B384 over the M3. The site had been leased in 1894 at £50 a year for seven years.[27] In 1909 the business was still in operation, but the brothers-in-law were supplementing their income by operating a delivery-service of goods and people from local railway stations.

Little is known of the brickyard in Chobham Park Lane which was managed by Mr Burningham, who went on to the new brick and tile works at Castle Grove, just south of Chobham, when this site closed.[28] The brick and tile works at Castle Grove were established in the early 20th century. In 1934 several kilns, drying beds, sludge beds and an engine shed are shown on the Ordnance Survey map. There was no evidence of any brickworks or extraction of gravel in 1896, and although by 1914 brick fields are noted with obvious signs of gravel extraction, only one or two very small buildings are shown, probably sheds, with no kiln marked on the site. Ernie Wells, a Chobham bricklayer, recalled that all clay was dug from the site. The clay would be extracted in the winter and was laid on the surface of the ground to allow the frost to get to it before bricks were made from it the following summer. According to Joy Mason, Castle Grove brick works closed in the late

1930s, although the site was still used to store materials until 1969 when the land was sold by auction. The map attached to the sale details shows the outline of the buildings on the site which had been partially destroyed by a fire in 1953.[29]

Many bricks were made on site in Surrey Heath as a house was built; clay would be dug from the site before building commenced which meant that bricks being made from it allowed the house to blend more naturally with its surroundings. When 116 acres of land in Bagshot was auctioned in 1859, it was described as 'a very eligible site for the erection of a mansion or gentleman's residence ... well calculated for building purposes and contains a large quantity of fine Brick Earth'.[30] The bricks were not used solely for building houses; when the Royal Military College was built at Sandhurst, the first batch of bricks, which failed, were made on site. Farm buildings were also made from home-made bricks and when George Wells built the *Red Lion* in Burrow Hill, he dug clay for them from near Killy Hill.[31] It is said that many of the large houses in Surrey Heath had ornamental ponds in their grounds where clay had been extracted to make bricks, and the resulting pit filled with water.

SAND, GRAVEL AND STONE WORKERS

Although sand, gravel and stone had been extracted from the heathland over the generations, this work became an entire industry, post-enclosure, with the building of large houses and the development of new roads to them. Traditionally, parishes needed gravel and small stones for the repair of roads. Larger sarsen stones were used to build churches, houses and for the ornamentation of brick-built structures including the bridges over the Basingstoke Canal. As with brick-earth, the lord of the manor had the right to issue licenses for the extraction of these materials. The stone at Chobham had been dug by those claiming commoners' rights even if they had none, so in 1857 the lord of the manor regularised the supply by issuing a lease to William Free 'to get dig and quarry the seams of stone lying in a certain portion of the waste in consideration of a yearly payment of £20'.[32]

39 Brickmakers Arms, *Chertsey Road, Windlesham*

40 *A sketch of a stone-cutter's cart*

SARSEN STONE

The composition of the local sarsen stone, and its uses, are defined in an undated document held at Surrey Heath Museum:

> These stones in many instances have been freed from their sandy matrix, and lie in the derivative gravels, in either a slightly or much worn state. Some have become ferruginous and friable; some retain their internal hardness. Occasionally the weathering had dissected them ... elsewhere these stones lie about on the surface of the country in large quantities and have been called 'grey wethers', since they look like sheep: and by the older name of 'Sarsdens' supposed ... to be of Saxon origin meaning 'sair'. These Sarsdens are sought for with an iron rod ... The deserted holes are dangerous pitfalls for man and beast.[33]

As the area was developed and land was cleared, specimens found in the gravels or railway cuttings were broken up, dressed and used for decorative masonry. According to Richard Wilson of West End, at anytime other than harvest you could find:

> A group of men busy at one of these sites digging as fast as they could. The block of stone would be slowly uncovered and found ... the men all the while to free it working up to their thighs in water for the heaths are very boggy ... As soon as they hoisted up the block of stone, usually by means of a rope or chain and pulley, the men would begin at once cutting it with a special saws into rough squares ... Saws were used, for while the sandstone was still wet and had not been exposed to the air, it was comparatively soft and easy to cut. That done the blocks were stacked up on the heath and soon had become as hard and as firm as any brick.[34]

Each village had a known area where the stone could be found.

Sarsens were also used as stepping-stones at Blackwater Bridge, and in 1727, John Ridges gave evidence in court regarding the upkeep of this bridge which forms the boundary of the three counties of Hampshire, Berkshire and Surrey. He had carted large stones to the crossing of the Blackwater, where they were laid as a causeway 'in order to be a stopp to step over to avoid the mud and dirt'.[35] Although a bridge already existed over the Blackwater river at this time, there was also a stepping stone walkway across water lying between the bridge and *The Harrow* (later the *Three Post Boys*) public house on the London Road in Yorktown. The first footpath known to have been paved in Surrey Heath was the stretch from the bridge near Hart Dene in Bagshot to The Cedars at the other end of the village, which was laid with local heath-stone, or sarsen stone, by 1770.

The local heath-stone, due to the lack of alternative building materials and the cost of the manpower to work it, was a valuable commodity. When James Lawrell purchased the Manor of Frimley from Henry Tichborne in 1789, he disputed the value of the estate and a long legal case began which itemised all aspects of income from the land. By 1789, 400 tons of stone were dug annually from the 'waste lands' within the Manor; the stone was valued at 2s. 0d. per ton, providing an income of £40 a year, when timber growing on the same estate was only valued at £20.[36]

Digging for local heath-stone, and repairing roads with it, was one of the tasks given by the Overseers of the Poor of Frimley to those out of work, and in 1834, the average daily rate given to the men was 1s. 6d.[37] It was seasonal work and when a new priority came along the men had to move on, as in Frimley in October 1826, when labourers were transferred from this task to begin trenching on the Duke of Gloucester's land on the border of Frimley and Bagshot.[38]

Another use for local stone was to line or edge the borders of the beds in the large gardens that were laid out, especially where alpines were grown. At Bagshot Park the gardeners referred to the stones as 'Bagshot diamonds' because of their hardness, and because when broken they usually consisted of colourless crystalline grains. A number of the stones had come from the nursery grounds, where the larger stones had had to be dragged out of the soil, as transplanting trees involved digging to a greater depth than ploughing land.[39]

A small quantity of one other stone was quarried, known as ironstone or 'ragstone' which was used to build Chobham Church. According to Ernie Wells, ironstone could be found on the common at Stanners Hill to the east of Chobham, where there are still potholes left behind from the extraction of the stone.[40]

SAND AND GRAVEL EXTRACTION

With the Enclosure Acts, allotments were set up for the poor and an area known to contain sand and gravel was set aside for use on the parish roads. In 1811, when the Enclosure Act for Windlesham was drawn up, the vestry clerk wrote explaining that there were already four pits in use in the parish: Curley Hill, Lavershot, Ribsden and Hatton Hill.[41] Post-enclosure there were pits on the Maultway, in Guildford Road in Frimley Green and on the Frimley fuel allotment. In addition to parish pits, there were also private pits where those allotted land sold the mineral rights. One of the private pits was on land east of Frimley Road, where Gordon Road

41 *Silica Works at Chobham*

stands today. Builders used the sand and gravel from local pits when building new houses, therefore, numerous pits were established as new areas developed, especially in Lightwater where there was a number of small gravel pits indicated on the maps in the early 20th century. Local Barton sand suitable for plastering and lime mortar were still taken from large pits as late as the 1930s when a 30ft-deep pit stood next to the Lupin Café on the London Road. The pits were usually refilled; occasionally, as this one was, with local refuse.[42]

Mr Lory of Bagshot, when recalling the building of the New Road to Windlesham, said it had been constructed in the 1840s, 'on faggots laid on what was virtually a bog. It had a gravel surface and by 1914 was in a very bad condition. During the 1914-18 War a surveyor named Bell ... practically rebuilt New Road finishing it in macadam and tarring the surface'.[43] It was during the First World War that many of the roads in Surrey Heath were surfaced with macadam rather than the traditional gravel. The resurfacing was not for the benefit of local residents, but for the smooth passage of military vehicles and troops.

On a site later occupied by Metco, at Burrow Hill to the north of Chobham, were the Silica Works where silica sand was extracted. Mr Tarrant, the Wentworth builder responsible for developing the large Wentworth estate at Sunningdale, had an interest in the works.[44] The silica sand was used for making glass and was later sold as a cleaning or abrasive substance by the name of Do-Do. For generations, before the common use of abrasive steel pads, local people had known the benefit of using sand to clean their cooking pots. It is believed the silica factory also produced a form of toothpaste during the First World War.

Chobham sand or silica was of a kind not found in many areas and in 1924 the Mersey Docks and Harbour Board applied to Lord Onslow for permission to dig eight tons of it. The letter stated they required this sand for research in connection with conserving the channels in the Mersey estuary, and that 'the only suitable sand for this purpose is to be obtained in the vicinity of Longcross Farm, Chobham'.[45] The Mersey Docks and Harbour Board were granted leave to dig for the Chobham sand, employing a Sunningdale company, Stearne & Sons, to extract it.

Masons and Stone Sawyers

Although cutting stone is not thought to have been practised much as a trade in its own right in Surrey Heath, there is one example in Frimley parish registers of a baptism in 1813 of the son of John Goodfellow, a stone sawyer. Goodfellow is not a local name and it may be that he had been employed in the building of the Royal Military College, which opened in 1812. The majority of the men working with stone would have been referred to as masons and, although this term does not appear in the early records for Surrey Heath, there were two such men: John Eades in 1820 and George Heartfree in 1833 working in Frimley.

One man who is well remembered locally for his work as a stone-mason is Henry Jesse Gomm, as he carried out much of the ornamental stonework in St Michael's Church at Yorktown. The *Camberley News* of 1915 contained his widow's obituary and it provides an insight into how people arrived in Yorktown. In a lengthy article, the newspaper noted that Henry Gomm was born at Great Berkhamsted, and was apprenticed as a stone carver in 1853 to George Myers, a builder of Lambeth, for three years at the age of 17 at a rate of 6s. a week the first year, 8s. the second year and 10s. the third year, plus food, lodging, clothing, washing and tools. Henry Gomm arrived in Yorktown in the early 1860s, probably to work on the Staff College, and was responsible for the eight carved medallions in St Michael's Church, Yorktown, and also the font at St George's Church in Camberley.[46] Henry's daughter, Ann Eleanor Gomm, was a Costumier at Corona House, Yorktown, who never married and left money for two houses to be built in Camberley for poor ladies. Miss Gomm's charity is still operating today.

Chimney Sweeps

Although this was not a traditional heathland trade, there were several chimney-sweeps working in the local villages in the 19th century who tended not to live within the confines of the village but on newly enclosed areas of heathland. Prior to the 19th century there is no mention in the local records of chimney sweeps, possibly because many villagers would have cleaned their own cottage chimney with a large bundle of gorse attached to a rope, which would have been inserted into the top of the flue and dragged down through the sooty hole by pulling on the rope. The trade subsequently became more widespread in Surrey Heath as local residents used coal rather than turf as their fuel. Coal was available locally after the Basingstoke Canal opened in 1794, and those with funds to purchase it would have been pleased with this alternative fuel. The main problem with the use of coal was that it left a thicker deposit in the chimney, which needed to be removed regularly. The men who took up the sweep trade in Surrey Heath appear to have been those who had led an itinerant life beforehand, or those who wished to earn a living rather than rely on charity. Examples in 1851 included William and Matthew Deane, who were born in Binstead, and were living at the top of College Ride near the Poor Allotment in Bagshot, and James Grainger, who lived on the edge of the village of Frimley Green at Mytchett. In 1881 Joseph Grainger was living at the Poor Allotment in Bagshot with his wife Martha and their eight children,[47] and Richard Bowyer was living in conditions described as 'poverty beyond description' in a cottage on the

42 *Mrs Godfrey or Grainger, the chimney sweep*   **43** *William and Mary Cole*

heath near Burrow Hill.[48] All of these families were poor but they were managing to live without applying to the Overseers of the Poor for handouts.

The Bagshot sweep Joseph Grainger, who was born in West End, had set up his business by 1871. He married Martha Grainger, whose family lived at Mytchett. The 1891 Census reveals that Joseph had died and Martha had married another sweep, Charles Godfrey, and they lived on the heath at the top of College Ride in Bagshot. Joseph Grainger's trade was described as bricklayer and chimney sweep, and when he died, his wife and their small son took over the business, the son being used as a climbing boy to scramble up the inside of the chimneys. Mrs Godfrey became a familiar sight, pushing a wicker pram through the village piled high with sooty brushes, and in Bagshot, she was also the village midwife and is referred to as Grainger or Godfrey.[49]

Other individuals became itinerant sweeps, moving from one village to another. One example was John Bath, who travelled throughout the local villages. John was enumerated as born in Winchester in the 1851 Census, although it's possible he could have been related to the Bath family from Burrow Hill in Chobham. John and his wife Caroline made their home in Surrey Heath from at least 1829, when they married at Chobham. In 1832, after the birth of their first two children, the Bath family was sent to the parish of St Mary, Southampton, possibly because they had become a burden to the Poor Rate, but they returned by 1833.[50] They had further children baptised at Chobham, Bisley and Windlesham as John moved around finding work.

In the late 19th and early 20th century the chimney sweep trade became a regular employment for men. With streets lined with new houses all burning coal, the new town of Camberley and villages of Frimley, Chobham, Windlesham and Bagshot could all support men taking up the trade.

Chapter Four

MILITARY USE OF THE HEATHLAND

EARLY TENTED CAMPS

As with all industry on the heathland, the movement of troops brought much-needed trade and opportunities for local residents. Military camps had been held on Bagshot Heath from the time of James I, and there were several reasons for this: the close proximity of Windsor and the Royal Lodge at Bagshot enabling the Royal Family to review their troops, the free-draining nature of the soil, and the fact that there were no field boundaries or crops growing on the land.[1] The use of Bagshot Park at the time of the Civil War was well documented, when a regiment of foot soldiers was stationed nearby from August 1643 until October 1645.[2] Diaries of the period give an idea of the numbers of men involved, with eight regiments of horses and the same number of foot soldiers containing between nine or ten thousand men: 'We came to Bagshotte where our City Brigade and Kentish Regiment were quartered in the Parke.'[3] Some provisions would arrive with troops but the inns, bakers, butchers and general provision merchants in Bagshot must have been overwhelmed with demand.

Most of the military camps held were located near Ascot, where the race-course had been established in 1711, and as the camps were held in the summer months they were usually delayed until after the main race-meeting at Ascot in June. Bagshot was also a popular site, especially as Bagshot Park was suitable quarters for those leading the men. In 1746 Johnson's Dragoons and Hawley's 'Ragged Fellows' were quartered at Bagshot, as Lord Albemarle, the Duke of Cumberland's aide-de-camp, was staying there.[4]

The open heathland between Ascot and Bagshot came to be regularly used for manoeuvres. In 1750, Fort Belvedere was erected at Shrubbs Hill as a 'belvedere', or lookout, for George II to view his troops encamped in Windsor Great Park and on Chobham Common.[5] In 1755 and 1756, Colonel Honeywell's and Colonel Woolf's troops were quartered at Bagshot and Windlesham, and in 1777 the Royal Horse Guards were at Ascot Heath.[6]

It is not clear how many troops attended the early military camps but there are entries in local parish registers which mention some of the men. The army was not as popular or as well-funded as the Navy and there was no permanent 'home' for them; the only way they could practise was to have mock battles at camps held

44 *Camp of 1792*

in the summer when men from all over the country would be able to travel to a suitable site. In 1788, with the threat from France, new army regiments were being formed and Bagshot Heath, Swinley, Ascot, Winkfield and Windlesham became the nursery ground for their training.[7]

In May 1792, the Duke of Richmond and Colonel Moncrieff surveyed the area around Bagshot for a summer camp for 7,000 and on 24 July, George III, accompanied by William Pitt, reviewed his troops at a site near Wickham Bushes between Bagshot and Bracknell.[8] In early August there were three days of manoeuvres when it was estimated that 50,000 people turned up to watch the troops. They would have travelled by coach, horse or on foot, with many sleeping overnight in their carriages near the camp. In the *Reading Mercury* a report included a reference to Sunninghill Wells, a hostelry and a place to 'take water', which in its day was a rival to the German spa towns, where officers had supper followed by dancing in the ballroom attached to the dining hall.[9] At this time the manoeuvres were much about promoting the army and hoping for public support and funding, and they encouraged as many people as possible to find their way there.

A map was produced by William Faden with the three sites for the army manoeuvres marked in red: the first was near Wickham Bushes, the second towards Hartley Wintney at Hartford Flats and the third near Caesars Camp at Aldershot.[11] Popular magazines gave their verdict on the event; *The Lady's Magazine* reported that when they arrived 'they may indeed be warranted in asserting to their friends that they saw a great deal of smoke, much dust, and many soldiers – but at a great distance'.[12] The proceedings were enhanced by men like the Duke of Richmond, who was attended by two footmen, both dressed in white. Reports in the *Public Advertiser* and the *Sunday Gazette* stated the King and Prince rode over daily from Windsor to observe the proceedings, however, the weather was extremely wet, and so their visits to the second phase of the camp at Hartford Bridge were curtailed and the troops moved back to Bagshot. The unsuccessful royal visit did not deter the production of a new comic opera entitled 'Hartford Bridge or the Skirts of a Camp' – no doubt a reference to the ladies accompanying the troops, described in the *Lady's Magazine* as 'well-dressed sprightly females' – which was playing at Covent Garden.[13] A new musical piece was also published at the same time, entitled 'Bagshot Heath Camp'. Both works were written to compensate those who were not able to visit the spectacle themselves; they must have had wide appeal as the opera was staged 36 times in 1792 at Covent Garden with Elizabeth Clendenning, or Clendillon, playing the lead role as Clara, and it was also replayed in 1793-4.[14]

During the final decade of the 18th century, annual camps were held at Bagshot. One of the largest camps was held in June 1800 when 30,000 men gathered just north of Windlesham for almost three months. The Commander-in-Chief of the army was the Duke of York, whose headquarters was at Bagshot Park.[15]

The disruption caused to daily life in local villages is not difficult to imagine; the influx of large numbers of men, horses, baggage carts and camp-followers would have had a huge impact on all the tiny villages surrounding this land, especially Windlesham, Frimley, Sunninghill and Chobham. The arrival of brightly-garbed army men meant a great deal of trade for the local shops and public houses, and was a temptation for sons to join up and for daughters to become smitten, as well as providing entertainment for all. On the down-side there was an increase in crime, drunkenness and destruction of the heath. In the parish registers for Windlesham in 1800 there were seven marriages of military men at the camp to women who were either local, or describing themselves as such.

Casualties at the mock skirmishes of local camps were inevitable, and some even occurred when men were off-duty. Oswald Werge, an officer in the 17th Light Dragoons, received a wound to his head when a riot broke out caused

45 *Sunninghill Wells: engraving of drawing*

46 *Army manoeuvres, Chobham 1907*

by high prices and lack of provisions.[16] Animals for slaughter would have been brought in on the hoof when the camp was set up, but to provide enough food for these men, the camp-followers and the horses was a mammoth task. As with the camp of 1792, the broadsheet producers were ready to profit from public interest in these events and a pamphlet was printed entitled *The Pie-man's Trip to Bagshot*.

Many soldiers were married, and as there was no permanent home camp, their wives and children travelled with them, even abroad. Nine burials took place at Chobham, and 13 at Windlesham Church during this three-month period in June 1800, including three women and two infants from the camp hospital.

With the troops return after the Peninsular wars, no further camps are noted until 1853.

DEVELOPMENT OF THE ROYAL MILITARY COLLEGE

With land values of heathland low in comparison to good farmland, and with the area being well-known as good military training ground, it was no surprise that local land was purchased for military use. The new Royal Military College, which was originally founded on a constricted site at Great Marlow, was built on land purchased by the Government in April 1801, the majority of which was in the Manor of Sandhurst, including the Manor House and farm buildings. John and Griselda Tekell (née Stanhope, the niece of Prime Minister William Pitt) had owned the land and it is said that Pitt purchased the land from John and Griselda and sold it on to the Government for three times what he had paid for it. The Government paid Pitt £9,966 12s. for 450 acres, the buildings and their contents. In June 1802 additional land south of the Wish Stream in Frimley was purchased from the Enclosure Commissioners for £1,357, and with a further purchase of 11 acres near Blackwater in July 1802, the Government held a total of just over 500 acres, 353 of which were heathland.[17]

In 1801 only 532 people lived in 97 dwellings in the whole of the Manor of Frimley and fewer in the village of Sandhurst. To build the vast military college, landscape the grounds and then staff the building and serve the Officer Cadets, a huge influx of new people were required to live nearby.[18]

The settlement which was built to house the new military college workers spread along the turnpike road from Blackwater Bridge to Frimley Road, and became known as New Town, Blackwater. The settlement soon took the name of York Town after the Duke of York, who was influential in the decision to

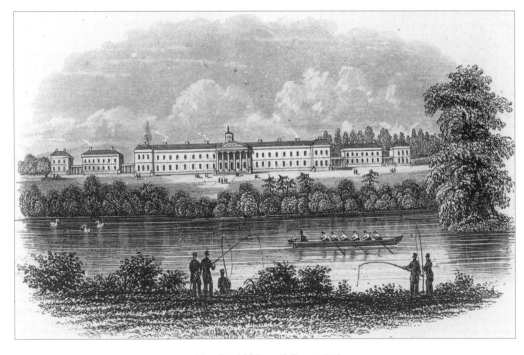

47 *Royal Military College, c.1865*

48   *Map of Chobham Camp, 1853*

house the college there, with other areas named Albany Terrace and Osnaburgh Hill, after two of his other titles. The main hotel on the corner of the Frimley Road was named the *Duke of York* by 1812 and the beerhouse *William IV* in Frimley Road was named after his brother. York Town was growing rapidly, and had a school, a doctor and shops along the one-sided high street which faced the source of its income; the college.

Initially those wishing to attend a Church of England service would have travelled to St Peter's at Frimley, to Sandhurst or to Hawley, but in January 1851 a new church was erected on land adjoining the college. This church, its vicarage, Yorktown School and the Drill Hall are the only permanent non-military buildings to this day that have been allowed to encroach on the grounds of the college.

The arrival of the college brought with it the 'crammers', that is, the schools to fast-track boys into the college. One of the first schools to arrive was opened by the Rev. James Pears who had been a member of the staff of the college at Great Marlow. In 1816 he purchased an old inn, *The Pelican*, at Windlesham and extended it to what is still known as today: Woodcote House School.

Chobham Camp of 1853

In 1850 the Duke of Cambridge was appointed as Commissioner to the Royal Military College and in 1852 became Inspector General of the Cavalry. Also in 1852, Prince Albert, the husband of Queen Victoria, became Colonel-in-Chief of the Rifle Brigade and Colonel of the Grenadier Guards. There was general

49 *Chobham Camp of 1853*

agreement between the Duke and the Prince that the army needed a summer camp for the practice of military manoeuvres. In 1847 Albert had suggested to the Duke of Wellington that a 'concentration of part of our land forces ... for practice and experience ... be held at Salisbury Plain, Winchester or Bagshot', but Wellington refused any suggestion that troops needed training.[19] The Duke died in September 1852 and he was given a magnificent funeral befitting the Hero of Waterloo, Commander-in-Chief of the British Army and Prime Minister of England. The opinion of his fellow officers was different in that they felt his:

> Acquiescence in the gradual decay of the Army, which, in the Peninsular War, he had with unremitting effort changed from an undisciplined, heterogeneous collection of units into as fine a fighting force as the world has ever seen, is incomprehensible ... [he] left this wreck of an Army as a terrible legacy to Lord Hardinge.[20]

The Duke of Cambridge reported on the state of the forces at this time and his report was truly damning. He found that there was no retirement age and the majority of the leading officers were aged between 68 and 88, with some men having been in service for up to 70 years. Very little military training had taken place since Waterloo, and the army were using outdated drill books from 1792. The army Regiments varied in size from 850 men up to 1,250 and were completely without any system of transport, supply or medical treatment.[21]

The result of the Duke of Cambridge's report was to concentrate the minds of the men in charge with rectifying obvious problems. Prince Albert, the Duke of Cambridge and Lord Hardinge were all aware that training of troops should take place as soon as possible, which meant the following summer. On 6 April 1853, Lord

50 *Aubrey Medhurst's shop*

51 *Benham's store, 1870s*

Hardinge wrote to Lord Onslow asking his permission for a camp to be held on his land as 'Chobham Common has been reported to be the most eligible ground for such an encampment'.[22] Lord Onslow agreed to the camp, but there was also the issue of the Commoners' Rights to the land, therefore, a vestry meeting was held where Lord Vaux of Highams, Sir Denis le Marchant of Chobham Place, Richard Collyer, William Daborn, James Ottaway, Mr Luker and Mr Baigent, all local men, were appointed to protect these rights. Lord Onslow had given parishioners part of the heath known as Great Portobello and Little Portobello Fields, just north of Burrow Hill, as a Parish Farm in 1815. One of the proposals at the vestry meeting was that stallholders who wished to sell refreshments should be offered plots on the Parish Farm land to provide a benefit to the poor; this was extended to a decision to rent out land surrounding the camp, with a charge dependant on how close it was to the action. The decision did not quell all opposition to the camp and when Lord Seaton, who was appointed Commanding Officer, moved to his H.Q. at Highams he received a visit from Richard Collyer, who represented the villagers. Lord Seaton wrote to Lord Hardinge informing him that although the villagers were originally against the idea of the camp they now 'were so convinced of the advantages to be derived from the quick sale of their Poultry; and also from the manure that would be collected after the departure of the Troops that no kind of General opposition or clamour would be made'.[23]

The camp on Chobham Common, like all others, had both advantages and disadvantages for local residents. Mr Benham, a grocer in Chobham, was appointed to supply provisions to the 1st Brigade of Infantry and the 38th and 93rd Regiments of Foot. 63 Constables and 14 Mounted Constables arrived in the village from

52 *Queen Victoria reviewing her troops, 1853*

the newly formed Surrey Police force and were lodged in Chobham, providing useful income for householders.[24] Local carriers were busy transporting people to and from the railway stations, and young boys collected the copper caps from the shot to sell to ironmongers. The old workhouse was utilised as a military hospital and the income from that, plus money paid for damage to the heath, was used to provide soup and bread for the poor.

Thousands of people flocked to the Chobham area, especially when Queen Victoria and Prince Albert attended the camp, and special trains were laid on to Woking, Sunningdale and Windsor. Chobham stationer William Aubrey Medhurst printed a guide to the camp, which was available at all railway stations. On 21 June, the day the Queen reviewed her troops, visitors arrived by every means available.

The main disadvantages of the Chobham Common camp were the disruption, overcrowding, drunkenness and the rise in crime, which must have worried householders, however, the main crime reported at Chobham was gambling. There were rules attached to the setting-up of the camp on Chobham Common prohibiting gambling booths being erected, but enforcement was extremely difficult, and wherever there was money to be made people moved in to take advantage. Chertsey Magistrates sat on 4 July when Robert Smith of Bristol was accused of setting up a gambling booth, which resulted in his goods being seized and the money used towards policing the camp.[25] On 9 August further problems arose when the *Iron Horse*, probably a gambling booth erected from galvanised metal, was identified as a house of 'Ill Fame', that is, of prostitution.[26] Later that month confirmation came that the *Iron Horse* was being operated as a brothel, with many officers and women there.

53-58 *Engravings of Chobham Camp*

Engravings of Chobham Camp, continued

After the summer camp on the Common broke up, Lord Hardinge's report stated that 'the novelty of Chobham had so generally drawn the attention of members of Parliament to the policy of repeating the experiment next year that I naturally waited till the camp broke up to collect the reports before I addressed the Government.'[27] Initially it is believed that part of Chobham Common was to be purchased for the sum of £15,000, for use as a permanent summer camp for the forces. While the camp was still operating, landholders in Chobham had applied for Acts of Parliament to enclose land, thereby making Chobham a less suitable site. Similar heathland at Aldershot, Farnham and Ash was compulsorily purchased by the Government. In Hardinge's confidential report of 26 September 1853 he noted that 27 Acts were passed on 20 August relating to Chobham, Aldershot and Farnham.[28] The criteria for land for military purposes included being free-draining land at a relatively cheap purchase price, within easy distance of a railway line to take the armed forces south for embarkation to Europe; this was the reason for the proliferation of military establishments in the Surrey Heath area. Hardinge makes it clear that the land at Aldershot was purchased for use as a summer camp for up to five months a year. As the shortcomings in training had become apparent after the campaign in the Crimea, it was essential that men were trained in all weathers, therefore Aldershot became a permanent camp: the 'Home of the British Army'.

Landmarks on maps produced of Surrey Heath in the 19th century relate to the tented camps in Surrey Heath. The landmarks include King's Beeches, where the King reviewed the troops, Wellington Bridge after the famous Duke and various redoubts or batteries on land between Chobham and Sunningdale.[29]

THE STAFF COLLEGE

With the return of officers from the Crimea, land adjoining the Royal Military College was identified by the Duke of Cambridge and Prince Albert as a suitable site for a new Staff College, not for young Officer Cadets as with the R.M.C., but for senior staff. The College was built on land north of the turnpike road from Bagshot to Blackwater and east of the Royal Military College, and once again, a new settlement grew up around it.

A few scattered cottages, plant nurseries and farms had been established on the heathland surrounding the site chosen for the Staff College after the 1801 enclosure, and by 1851 the area was known as Mudd Town.[30] With the building of the College coinciding with the purchase of land from the executors of John Tekell by Captain Charles Raleigh Knight, a new town (known today as Camberley) was laid out in a grid pattern opposite the college entrance. From 1862 when the college opened, until 1877 when the railway arrived, the village was known as Cambridge Town after the Duke of Cambridge. The town's name was changed to Camberley on 15 January 1877 in an attempt to avoid the confusion between this new town and Cambridge, which had frequently caused the post to go astray. Once again, as at Yorktown 50 years before, the new town of Camberley attracted men to provide labour and services for the military, including a number of laundries. Until Camberley Railway Station opened, the London Road was the main trading area. The trading area comprised of an almost completely one-sided 'high street'

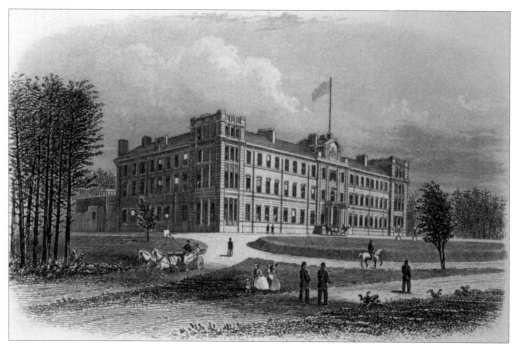

59 *Staff College, c.1865*

from the *Cambridge Hotel* to Blackwater Bridge, with a large school between them supplying the needs of children from both Yorktown and Camberley. The current High Street was initially lined with houses. It was only after 1877, when people started to use it to walk to the railway station, that shop fronts were added to the houses that initially lined the High Street, and the land between was then filled with purpose-built shops.

MILITARY TRADESMEN

People moved to Camberley and Yorktown to provide services to the military – the first substantial industry in Surrey Heath. Some of those who came were formerly providing services to the college at Great Marlow, and included the bootmaker, or cordwainer, John Stallwood, who is buried in grave number one at St Michael's Church. Tradesmen could find work close to any large establishment, and within a few years men with trades as diverse as armourers, training grooms, clerks, sutlers, bedmakers, bandmasters and cooks were all settling here. These were traditional trades in all villages, but along with that of the bootmaker they were occupations especially prominent among those providing a service to the military.

TAILORS AND DRESSMAKERS

As soon as the college opened in 1812 military tailors were required, and by 1841 there were a cluster of men working in Yorktown. Spaced-out along the London Road opposite the Yorktown gate were workshops employing 15 men enumerated

60 *Harry Salt's shop, livery maker to the Duke of Connaught*

as tailors.[31] Only Job Jones, of all of these men, was born in Surrey. Most of these tailors had moved on again by 1851, leaving John Farrell, Thomas McCrery and the Cayley brothers to establish firms which lasted into the next century. The larger businesses also employed journeymen and in 1851 in Yorktown there were 12 journeymen tailors.

With the growth in the number of establishments in Surrey Heath, whether military or orphanages, sanatoriums or asylums, a uniform was required; and this opportunity attracted many young businessmen to the area. At the beginning of the 20th century tailoring was still a trade offering good long-term prospects, despite the rise in ready-made clothing stores. Farrell's, the military tailors in Yorktown, applied to retain men due to be drafted into the army in 1916 as they were wholly engaged in making uniforms. Some men however, did have to join the army and, by May 1917, 14 of Farrell's employees had seen action, three of them had lost their lives and one had won a D.C.M.[32]

For a woman, working with a needle was the easiest of tasks open to her if she had been left a widow and did not wish to end up 'in service' or if she needed additional income when rearing small children. Not all women had the aptitude or the eyesight for sewing and it was a tiring and poorly paid trade in Surrey Heath. Groups of women lodging in Yorktown were offering to work as bonnet, dress or mantua makers (a mantua was a loose gown in one piece from shoulder to hem, worn over a petticoat and open down the front). As far as is known, there were no tailor's shops that employed women, nor women's workshops, until the late 19th century when they were employed in Yorktown working button-holes on uniforms, and in some cases adding braid or stitching military emblems. As the area developed more opportunities for social and cultural events arose, providing additional employment to women able to offer dress and bonnet-making services.

MILITARY BOOTMAKERS

The role of the military boot- or shoemaker was a specialised trade. As with a general shoemaker, the wooden last for each customer had to be made before work on the footwear could begin. A constant round of new customers made last-making a perpetual task, unlike most village shoemakers where a last would give a pattern for a customer's footwear for many years. Military boots had to be suitable for riding as well as for training or manoeuvres, and were almost knee-high so each had to be supple as well as strong around the calf. In addition to the boots for general military-wear, there were also dress-uniform boots made from finer leather, all were hand-stitched, and occasionally this stitching work was given to women to finish.

John Stallwood moved to Yorktown from Great Marlow to provide military boots for the cadets when the Royal Military College opened in 1812; there followed in his wake a large body of men. In the 1841 Census almost all of these men were newcomers to the area.[33] John Stallwood had his shop on the corner of Frimley Road and the London Road with James Shaw, George Stephens and William Christy in the same building and along the main London Road were a further 11 tradesmen who were employing the only named apprentices in Surrey Heath at this time: George Stokes and Henry Jones, aged 15, and Charles and Thomas Webb, aged 15 and 14.

61 *Stallwood bootmaker's shop, 1930s*

BY APPOINTMENT
TO THE

ROYAL
MILITARY COLLEGE.

TRAVISS BROS.,
YORKTOWN, SURREY,
GENERAL IRONMONGERS & SMITHS,
*Gas, Water and Range Fitters, Electric and Ordinary Bell-Hangers,
Locksmiths.*
KITCHEN UTENSILS REPAIRED AND RE-TINNED.
**Lawn Mowers ground and repaired. Sewing Machines, Tricycles,
Bicycles and Models made and repaired.**

62   *Traviss advertisement, 1889*

MILITARY BLACKSMITHS AND FARRIERS

With all military men arriving at the colleges by horse or by carriage, and with
training in equestrian excellence a major aspect of training the cadets, a large number
of blacksmiths and farriers were also attracted to the Surrey Heath area. Work
in housing the horses owned by the cadets was also available, and livery stables
were established opposite the colleges; this was in addition to the general trade
the farriers received from being close to the turnpike road. George Traviss was
trading in Yorktown in 1838 and by 1842 a number of men had set up in business,
including James Hunt and his son George, with premises at Osnaburgh Hill.

Blacksmiths and farriers relied heavily on the patronage of the Royal
Military and Staff College. In 1889 William Bartlett with his smithy in Park Street,
Camberley, and the Traviss Brothers at Yorktown, were advertising that they were
'By Appointment' to either college with the royal crest of appointment at the centre

63   *Gates made at Bartlett's forge, Frimley Green*

of their advertisement.[34] The Bartlett family arrived a little after the Traviss family, one with businesses in Farnborough and Frimley Green and another with premises in Yorktown and Camberley. The smithy in Camberley appears to have been established just after the Staff College was built, as William Bartlett advertised that the business was founded in 1863.[35]

As the Surrey Heath area developed, younger men arrived to set up businesses. Albert Cudlipp, one of the younger sons of Benjamin Cudlipp the Bagshot blacksmith, moved to Camberley in 1895, setting up his forge just off Princess Street.[36] At Frimley Green in the 1880s, Henry Ransom had purchased the blacksmiths shop set up by Thomas Traviss before the influx of military men. In the 1890s, Ransom's shop was taken on by William Deeks, who was able to pass on a thriving trade to his son in the early 20th century, especially as Deepcut and Pirbright were now busy with troops. As business was brisk, a second forge in Frimley Green Road was opened by another William Bartlett, who had been a farrier in the army for 13 years. In the First World War

64   *Bartlett's forge, Camberley High Street*

65   *First petrol pump at Deeks Garage, Frimley Green*

66 *Bartlett's ironmongery shop, Camberley High Street*

Bartlett rejoined the Army Veterinary Corps, employing George Agar to keep his forge working. George was almost fully employed working on military horses and pack-mules.[37]

As the trade evolved, William Deek's son turned his craft to mechanical innovations and opened a garage at the front of the forge, introducing the first petrol pump to the village and running a taxi service in a car often driven by his wife. The third generation of the family, Vic Deeks, continued with this range of skills, usefully applying them to running this garage and the sale and repair of bicycles.[38]

There are no longer any blacksmiths employed as farriers for the army in Surrey Heath, but memories do remain. Ivy Potten recalled visiting her father's forge in Camberley High Street when she was a child:

67 *Frimley High Street and forge*

To see him lift his strong arms to work the bellows, and then to hold the long iron tongs to pull out the red hot horseshoe ... The sound of the two metals meeting, made a resounding ringing tune. The brilliant sparks would fly like stars from his hammer and we would edge back to the door; but Father knew his job too well to cause us any danger.[39]

Later Military Tented and Permanent Camps

Although three major sites, Aldershot, the Royal Military College and Staff College, were now permanently used for the army, local heathland was still used for exercises and for summer tented-camps.

Over the centuries, provisions and equipment would have been carted for these occasional camps on loaded wagon-trains. With the opening of the Basingstoke Canal goods were carried by barge as far as Frimley Wharf where they could be transferred to carts. Deepcut, Pirbright and Mytchett were all training-grounds for the army by the late 19th and early 20th centuries. As it had been in Bagshot and Chobham, men would be housed for military manoeuvres in tented camps for the duration of the exercises prior to the establishment of more substantial accommodation and administration blocks. It was the opening of the Basingstoke Canal that enabled the material to be transported for the building of the barracks at convenient heathland locations along its route; North Camp, Aldershot, and later Mytchett, Pirbright, Deepcut and Church Crookham barracks were all built near the canal. At Pirbright, 3,070 acres of heathland, almost three quarters of that parish, were purchased by the War Office, and the guards camp was erected in 1892, enlarged in 1894 and re-built in 1902.[40] The original buildings on all of the barracks sites were predominately made of wood – the wooden huts were a fire hazard as they were tarred and felted and rather close together so that iron sheets on wheels had to be hauled into place to stop fire spreading from one hut to another.[41]

Despite the land owned by the military authorities in Frimley and Camberley in the 20th century, the army were still using Chobham Common as a site for

68   *Royal Military and New College*

summer exercises in the 1920s. The Guards Brigade had 'for more than 30 years had exclusive use of' it;[42] later they were substituted by other soldiers from Pirbright. Lord Onslow was concerned as he feared the heath would be damaged, therefore, special measures were put in place to protect the heath from fires. Soldiers were allowed to smoke but not light fires; no horses or artillery were to be ridden over the heath; and no guns could be placed on cricket pitches, golf greens or young plantations – clearly indicating how the area had changed from the Camp of 1853. The soldiers were also barred from cutting trees, brushwood, fern and furze and no trenches were to be dug.

Deepcut camp was built on land owned by the Pain family of Frimley Green, who had purchased much of the area from Ashmoor Road (Wharf Road today) to Colony Gate on the Maultway in the 1860s and erected a number of large dwellings. It appears from the outset that the family had wished to sell off a large portion of their land, as land was becoming more valuable, with both the nursery industry and the army finding it suitable for their purposes. In March 1882 Arthur Pain drew up a plan to portion off the estate into 105 large plots to be sold for housing, with the lake at the side of the canal (now part of Lakeside complex) as a feature for all to appreciate.[43] Nothing came of the proposal and in 1894, the eastern edge of the land was sold to the War Department for £20,250 for building Blackdown and Deepcut barracks with the remainder nearer Frimley Green being sold for housing.[44] Several of the houses erected by the Pain family in Deepcut were appropriated for military use, including Fairseat, Overdale, Huntspill and Blackdown House.[45]

A Camberley builder, James Knight, purchased land opposite Deepcut camp in the early 20th century and was responsible for laying out new roads and building

69   *Eton boys training on Chobham Common, 1905*

70 *Post Office in Frith Hill Camp*

many shops along Deepcut Bridge Road, along with civilian housing in adjacent streets. The new roads, shops and houses provided short-term work for the building trades and longer-term employment for those who worked in tea-rooms, the cinema, the post office and general shops opposite the camp.

In the autumn of 1889 the Rifle Range moved from Wimbledon to its new site on heathland between Bisley and the guards camp at Pirbright. Initially it was a tented camp, but by the following year a branch railway from Brookwood Station served the site with its Bisley Bullet bringing in visitors, and gradually more substantial buildings were erected. Local boy Harry Poulter, who lived near the *Jolly Farmer* at Camberley, wrote in his diary in July 1890 about his first visit to the 'New Wimbledon':

> Up Heatherside to Colony Gate where we saw the red flags so we had to go round Pirbright through the Guards Camp over the rough heath through part of the bogs and then we came to the new camp … The royal train came in about half past 4 o'clock we were in the front so we had a good view of the Prince and Princess of Wales … The Princess of Wales fired the shot and hit No 12 target.[46]

71 *Ablutions at Mytchett Camp*

Large numbers of people were employed when the camp was in full operation; it took a staff of 12 post office workers to man their tent alone in 1919.

FIRST AND SECOND WORLD WAR CAMPS

At Mytchett, the land surrounding Mytchett Place was another site for summer camps. Built for the Hollest family in the early 19th century, Mytchett Place was sold by George James Murray to the War Department in March 1912 for a sum of £16,500, and the site was used for tented camps in the First World War for officer training.[47] A series of postcards were produced of Mytchett camp, showing serried ranks of tents. Young officers had to use improvised outdoor sculleries and washed and shaved in open-air ablution facilities. After the First World War, the Military Foot Police were housed in hutments from 1920 and by 1934 stables, married quarters and officers' quarters covered the area between the railway line and Mytchett Lake.[48] The main building, known as Keogh Barracks after Sir Alfred Keogh, Royal Army Medical Corps Director in the First World War, was built in the mid-1930s with the Army School of Hygiene built slightly later in 1939. Surprisingly, perhaps because of its later date, there was no commercial development around the camp as there had been with Deepcut, though some residents of Mytchett did obtain work in the grounds of the camp as domestic staff. Although it was well-known among the local population that its most-famous war-time visitor, Rudolf Hess, was held at Mytchett Place from 20 May 1940 until 26 June 1942, none saw him.[49]

During the First World War, a camp was set up on the heathland at Frith Hill, between Deepcut and Heatherside, where German and Austrian aliens and prisoners-of-war were held. In May 1915, a report in the *Camberley News* confirmed that there were between fifteen and sixteen hundred men at the Frith Hill camp, with more coming in every week.[50] The men were housed in tents surrounded by a

72   *Cooking and cleaning at Mytchett Camp*

73   *Troops at Frimley Station in the First World War*

74   *Hess was held here in Mytchett Place during the Second World War*

75   *Frith Hill Camp*

barbed-wire fence with sentry points around the perimeter and each Sunday a local police officer had to be on duty to control the number of people coming to the site to peer at them. One of these visits was recorded in Vera Brittain's *Chronicle of Youth* when she made a visit to the camp with her friend Cora on the 24 September 1914. She said it was 'as if one were going to the Zoo … [the crowds] so numerous one could hardly see the thoroughfare'. One of the many civilians held at Frith Hill was a commercial artist named George Kenner, who sketched daily-life under canvas. Several of his paintings are now held at Surrey Heath Museum.

The prisoners held at Frith Hill were engaged in work parties, including helping the Canadian troops to erect Deepcut Railway Station, a branch line from Bisley Camp built to bring in troops and goods. The construction of the railway provided another use for the abundance of pine trees in the area as the Booking Office at the station was made from them, and in photographs of the interior, which included a splendid newspaper and tobacconist shop, the table and the benches were also made from pine.

The great influx of military men living locally and passing through Surrey Heath could make for difficult conditions in local villages during the First World War. The *Camberley News* reported streets full of drunken troops. In January 1915, 100 military drivers passing through the village of Bagshot were billeted on the inhabitants overnight.[51] Many of the large houses in Camberley and Windlesham were requisitioned as Military Hospitals at a time when retaining staff to manage them was extremely difficult. Nursing staff generally lived in, but some boarded with local people. The Priory at Frimley, Firlands and Heatherbank in Camberley, Windlesham Moor and the largest, Windlesham Military Hospital, all housed men injured at the front.

Local tradesmen were encouraged to join the army at the recruiting office in Camberley as they were required as harness-makers, saddlers, shoeing-smiths and wheelwrights in the Army Remount Department, with a wage of between 1s. 5d.

and 5s. a day. The recruiting office were also offering work for 16 cycle fitters.[52] Other people found employment at the Royal Aircraft Factory at Farnborough, where women were employed in painting canvas used for planes.

Men returning from war with military expertise in bootmaking, tailoring or photography settled down in business, advertising their association with the army with pride and benefiting from contracts awarded to them; this was perhaps a good move as there were so many officers retiring to Camberley from the army that by the 1930s it was known as Colonelstown. Typical of the reports in the national press is the following: 'Colonels by the score weave and wobble in and out of traffic on their cycles … you can't walk in the High street without bumping into a brace of brigadiers or spotting a general in a fish queue.'[53]

Post-war there was still extensive use of heathland for military manoeuvres, and as tanks and other mechanical vehicles came into use, much of the land was utilised for testing them. Today, tank-testing facilities still exist near Red Road. The *Camberley News* in 1926 reported that Dominion and Colonial troops were demonstrating their skills to the War Office in how to manoeuvre tanks over difficult terrain.[54] In this instance, the War Office inspected the tanks on Old Dean Common and then went to the grounds of the R.M.C. to watch the erection of a bridge over the lake which would support the weight of a tank.

The Second World War brought its own crop of tented 'villages' on the heath, which were made more permanent by the eventual erection of Nissan huts. On Old Dean Common men were initially housed in tents after Dunkirk, the site becoming most famously, the home of the Free French in the Second World War, with Lorraine School and Lorraine Road commemorating their stay. The French were present in town for almost four years and became a familiar sight; Charles de Gaulle would be seen at times striding around Camberley, and the men played in

76 *First World War: injured soldiers in Yorktown*

77-78   *Free French on Old Dean Common*

79 *War memorial and entrance to colleges*

football matches against local sides and trained on the adjoining heath. The Free French flew in and out from Blackbushe, an airport developed during 1942 for wartime use, which would eventually provide work for many men in the burgeoning airline industry in the late 1950s and early 1960s. Eagle Airways, Staravia and Dan Air were three of the companies that flew from here.

At Chobham, near Brick Hill, a hutted camp was built for Canadians, and taken over by the British Army. When the army left in 1945, the huts to the north of the Chertsey Road were occupied by local families anxious for a place to live, and those on the south were occupied by German prisoners-of-war, including Bert Trautmann, the footballer who subsequently played for Manchester City.

Many large houses were requisitioned during the Second World War for military use: part of Frimley Park House became a maternity ward, with another wing being used as a convalescent home for officers. Warren House at Frimley was used as a NAAFI. The majority of large houses were utilised as overflow accommodation for the military, including Watchetts House, which was occupied by Canadians.[55] Beaufront, in Portsmouth Road, Camberley, was used by the Auxiliary Training Services (ATS) and it was here that Princess Elizabeth received her training. Young ladies were taught how to change tyres and drive a truck in the grounds of the old Cordwalles School, now the site of Collingwood College.[56]

Some large dwellings were used for industrial purposes: the Grange at Chobham housed workshops for making bomb-aiming equipment, and Dakota aircraft parts were made at Wood Hall in Westwood Road, Windlesham. Establishments such as The Grange and Wood Hall proved vital at time of war, as with little industry the area was not a major target for German bombers. Several small firms were able to move out of more heavily-bombed areas and set up in Camberley on land just off Frimley Road, providing the first wave of our post-war light industry.

The College at Sandhurst today is known as the Royal Military Academy, which is the result of an amalgamation of two colleges in 1947: the Royal Military College, which trained cavalry and infantry, and the Royal Military Academy, formerly at Woolwich, for engineers, signals and artillery officers. Today, the former Staff College building is used by the Army Medical Services Corps following the setting-up of the Tri-Services College at Shrivenham.

Military establishments no longer surround the Surrey Heath area. Deepcut Camp has closed and is now a modern housing estate, but has retained the names of old battles: Alma and Dettingen. Local people no longer rely on 'serving the army', but there is still the legacy of an occasional military tailor working in our midst, and the sound of gunfire as those training practise on the heathland.

Chapter Five

THE INFLUENCE OF THE TURNPIKE ROAD

HIGHWAYMEN

The legendary 'trade' associated with Bagshot Heath was that of highwayman. Over the past few years many notable men of the road have been shown to be just legends, including Parson Darby. Until very recently, we would have spoken in confidence of William Davis, better known as the Golden Farmer. In truth it now seems that, although there was a William Davis who was tried at the Old Bailey for robbery in 1685, he was not the Golden Farmer; this was John Bennet alias Freeman. William Davis was of the Parish of St Giles and he was tried and sentenced to death in 1685 for stealing a silver tankard. In September 1689 the *London Gazette* described the Golden Farmer, alias Freeman or Hill (not Bennet in this instance), as 'an indifferent, tall, black Man, well set, with black hair, has a shaking in his Head, and is between 50 and 60 years of age'.[1] In December 1690, 'John Bennet alias freeman, but more notoriously known as the Golden Farmer was tried for the Murther of Charles Taylor.' It was this John Bennet alias Freeman, accompanied by others said to be accomplices of William Davis, including Old Mob, who carried out several attacks on travellers that ended in murder. It has always been rather a mystery why *The Golden Farmer* would have set up a farm on what has always been the edge of Bagshot heath, land totally unsuited to most farming in the 17th century other than for grazing a few hardy sheep, when there was land nearby more fertile. It is probable that John Bennet acquired his nickname from his habit of 'farming' gold from travellers.

The Golden Farmer tavern, which it is said was formerly Davis's farmhouse, was probably just a beerhouse built along the very busy stretch of road along the edge of Bagshot Heath at the time, or just after, the Golden Farmer was hung in a gibbet on Bagshot Heath. Richard Lapthorne wrote a newsletter at the time that 'on 26th December 1690 John Bennet … the notorious offender the Goulden Farmer was executed according to warrant in Fleet Street and his body hangs in chaynes on Bagshot Heath'.[2] A broadsheet entitled *The Golden Farmer's Last Farewell*, illustrated with a woodcut of John Bennet hanging in the gallows, was published by P. Brooksby, and made him notorious; the hill where his body hung in a gibbet became known as the Golden Farmer Hill.[3] Writing several years later in 1719, Captain Alexander Smith confused the story by stating that The Golden Farmer,

80 *Turnpike gate at Yorktown*

named by him as Davis, was tried in 1690 and 'hanged in chains on Bagshot Heath opposite his house'. As Davis had been executed in 1685, and as no one by the name of Davis was tried in 1690 for any crime associated with the highway, it was obviously a mistake which has been repeated over the generations. It seems the only local highwayman story known to be reasonably true is that of Claude Duval.

EMPLOYMENT ON THE ROADS

Although not directly related to the heathland, the vast majority of the service industries in Surrey Heath came about through the nature of the land. The first of the service industries was the road system which brought travellers needing food and shelter. The main route from London to the West Country cuts across the northern tip of the borough, and the Roman road with a parallel route north of the London Road has carried travellers for generations. Prior to the creation of the turnpike road (London Road and Portsmouth Road today), a network of paths and lanes

81 Jolly Farmer *named after the Golden Farmer highwayman*

82 *Carriage traffic at Sunningdale, c.1903*

would have criss-crossed the heath, converging at fords across rivers such as Blackwater, leading to oases of shelter like Bagshot with its Royal hunting lodge and taverns. All of the industries that supported the road system provided much needed employment, and Bagshot of all the villages profited most.

The service trades associated with daily life were the same as for all villages: bakers, grocers, chandlers, shoemakers, innkeepers and blacksmiths, plus the extra services due to the busy road through Bagshot of ostlers and post-chaise drivers. Postboys carrying sacks of letters were eventually replaced by receivers and postmen. Trades which flourished in Bagshot alone also existed, primarily associated with the coach trade. In 1828, according to a list of coaches produced by C.C. Wetton of Egham, numerous conveyances with wonderful names were passing through at all hours of the day and night.[4] Coaches going to Southampton included the *Nimrod*, *Telegraph*, *Independent* and the *Union*, the *Heavy Coach* and the *Royal Mail*, whilst others went to smaller destinations, including *Mr Monk's*, which passed daily to Odiham, and *Collyer's Safety* to Alton. In 1832

83 *Bagshot Square,* Kings Head *on right*

84   *Empty roads in Bagshot following the decline in coach trade*

advertising regarding Bagshot still stated 'London coaches call at the *King's Arms* or the *White Hart Inns* every hour during the day and several coaches call at the *Bell and Crown* during the night.'[5] In addition, Bagshot men operated a carrier service with John Hockley taking goods to Guildford each week, and Reading once a fortnight. William Taylor carried goods to London each Monday and Thursday and wagons travelled to Southampton, Winchester and Exeter every day. This was the final stage of a way of life which had supplied an income for generations of men, as the arrival of the railway caused the coach-trade to decline rapidly.

TOLLS AND TOLL-HOUSES

The turnpike road that passed through Bagshot and split into two separate roads at the top of Jenkins Hill provided direct employment for people of Bagshot and Frimley as gate-keepers or road-labourers. Three main local gates were situated just west of the *Cricketers* public house in Bagshot, in the centre of Frimley Street and on the London Road in Yorktown near the corner of Laundry Lane.

John Knight of Farnham recalled that in his early days (he was born in 1847) coaches, carriages and wagons had no brakes; as they headed down an incline they had to apply a drag bat, which 'would often cut up the road in a most ruthless manner',[6] making work for those who had to repair the surface, a task often given to the very poor or men receiving parish assistance. William Albert, in *The Turnpike Road System in England 1660-1840*, gave accounts of whole family groups being occupied in repairing roads, organised by a local surveyor. Albert gave the rate of pay for the Mile-Men in the 1820s as 12s. a week, while a labourer working with them received 10s. a week.[7] In May 1813, an advertisement appeared in the *Reading Mercury* for the 'Auction of the Repairs of the said Roads for the term of three years' by the Trustees of the Turnpike from the *Golden Farmer* at Bagshot to

Swallowfield.[8] The first stretch of road to be let was that from the *Golden Farmer* to the middle of Blackwater Bridge.

Some men made their living as 'toll-farmers', and would make an offer for the income for a set period hoping they could make a profit. The right to the tolls collected from the Frimley Gate were auctioned at *The Bush* in Farnham.[9] The Frimley gate, in 1788, was producing an income of just over £178 a year, with a charge for each horse passing both ways at 1d. a time. Exemption from payment of the tolls was granted to farmers taking their produce to market or for villagers on their way to church. In the *Reading Mercury* in October 1839, the Trust advertised the 'tolls arising at the tollgate and weighing engine upon the turnpike road leading from the 20-mile stone on Egham Hill to a place called Basingstone, near the town of Bagshot, called or known by the name of Bagshot Gate and Weighing Engine'.[10]

Gate-keepers were paid quite substantial wages for the time; although none are quoted for this Trust, at Kilburn they were paid 14s. a week in 1820, and this was in addition to a house or cottage which came free with the position. Locally, gate-keepers were also provided with bedding and fresh mattresses. The men, or occasionally women, who collected the tolls at the gates were housed in adjoining cottages as they had to be on duty 24 hours a day.

Local toll-gatherers, or toll-gate keepers, at Yorktown were John Chandler in 1814, and Richard Withers and Thomas Archer in 1827.[11] From 1832, Richard Withers was assisted by Ann West, who was living in a cottage opposite him. Daniel Jerome and William Hall were identified as 'Gate Keepers' in the 1851 Census at Frimley, with James Guest the 'Tollgate Road labourer' living next to William Hall. Mr and Mrs Jerome, later gatekeepers at Frimley, were recalled in George Sturt's *A Farmer's Life* when he described 'Mr Jerome the keeper of it, a little short, very stout man. And his wife was just such another, only more so. Such a nice kind woman … Invariably after Ann had gone through, Mrs Jerome had a bunch of flowers for her'.[12] At Bagshot, however, it is more difficult to identify the staff employed. In *Robson's Commercial Directory* of 1838, William Graham is listed at 'The Cricketers – Bagshot Gate' and in 1874, at the very end of the tollgate system, Mrs Sarah Smith appears in the *Post Office Directory* as the keeper.

Toll-houses were small lodges abutting the road, and as that used by Richard Withers at Blackwater was in a poor state and rather damp by 1843, it was proposed that a new dwelling should be built for him, but Mr Parfett, the brewer who owned the land, refused an offer for the site. The Trustees decided to alter, adapt and ventilate the existing lodge used by Richard Withers to make it habitable.[13] In December 1869, it was resolved by the Bagshot Odiham and Alton Turnpike Trust that the Yorktown gate would be taken down, and the land on which the building stood offered to the Royal Military College.[14] Although the toll-gates appear on the local O.S. maps of 1871, the survey for the map was carried out in the late 1860s at the very end of the period in which tolls were extracted.

INNS

Inns in the Surrey Heath area were of such variety, size and standard that to try to briefly summarise them is impossible. Little record exists of the local beerhouses except in journals and diaries of travellers, or in court records when a crime was

85   Three Mariners *and* Bridge House *public houses, Bagshot*

committed. Inns and beerhouses changed their names almost as often as they changed ownership, and it is especially difficult to trace the history of the Bagshot inns prior to the 18th century due to the lack of manorial records. The largest inns, all named the *White Hart*, were at Frimley, Chobham and Bagshot. The *King's Arms* and the *Bell* at Bagshot are also well-known. Few records exist of *The Victory* or the *Duke of Wellington* in Bagshot; or of the *Wagon & Horses*, *Running Mare* and *The Bear*, which were all advertised for sale in Chobham in 1813.

The majority of local inns and beerhouses had a few acres of land to tend, as well as offering food, ale, a bed and stabling for the horses. The largest, or most prestigious establishment, was the *King's Arms* at Bagshot. The entrance gates to the hotel were described by Lord Torrington in his diaries in 1782 as 'very antique, loaded with iron, and would and might, have defended a fortress'.[15] Other later hostelries rivalled the *King's Arms*, especially the *White Hart*, the contents of which were auctioned in 1839, when the coach trade was in decline. The list of items to be sold along with the *White Hart* included '20 fast and very superior Post Horses, 3 Post Chaises, a Gig, 10 sets of excellent Harness, 17 four-post and tent beds and furniture, 5 Stump beds and 22 excellent goose-feather beds.'[16] Also included with the sale of the *White Hart* were mahogany dining tables with shifting leaves, Brussels and Kidderminster carpets, sofas, chimney-glasses, dozens of ale and wine glasses, copper saucepans and the contents of the linen cupboard.

Inns offering accommodation would usually have provided an overnight service for travellers. An example of the facilities offered to someone staying at an inn a little longer comes from the diary of Edward Ryde, a surveyor employed at Chobham, who arrived at *The Sun* in January 1844. Ryde initially paid a day-rate and on 19 February he records 'Agree with Mr Squires that he shall charge and I will pay

86 The Sun *at*
    Chobham

25/- per week for my board and lodging exclusive of anything I may drink except Beer at Dinner'.[17] Mr Squires also made money from Ryde playing games of skittles, for which he pocketed 10d., and for supplying a horse and ostler at the rate of 2s. 6d. a day. Breakfast was taken at any time between 7.30 and 8.30 am, and for an earlier start, a meal of cold eggs and lemonade was set out for 5am. Ryde's diary states that he would call in for lunch if near enough to the inn and dinner would be taken at any time from 4pm until 7pm. On occasion, Edward Ryde would entertain friends, including local tailor Mr Rowland, a builder called Jeremiah Howard, and members of the Waterer family. On 19 March the village must have been very busy as he wrote 'John Waterer again spends the day with me and Mr Squires. Beds all being engaged sleeps with me.'[18]

It was not uncommon for guests to share a room with a stranger, especially in lower-class inns, and by the 19th century there were common lodging houses in Bagshot to cater for the poorer clientele. All classes were known to pass through local inns, and when the *King's Arms* at Bagshot was advertised to let in 1839 it boasted that it was 'countenanced by Royalty and the first Nobility'.[19] The inn had two parlours, four best bedrooms and two for travelling servants, as well as a dressing-room, a good kitchen and dairy. With stabling and a coach-house, plus a walled garden where produce could be grown for the table, a granary and three plots of pasture for grazing horses, the *King's Arms* was available at an extremely low rent, which was probably a last-ditch attempt to attract a new licensee at a time when trade was declining. In the same year, coach companies trading from Reading were offering reduced rates for travel to offset the attraction of the new rail service. The *White Hart* in Bagshot was offered to let in 1839, and it was advertised to appeal to a wider range of trades, including postmasters, at a reduced rate.[20]

BEERHOUSES

The Beerhouse Act of 1832 had allowed householders to brew and retail beer from their own homes, provided they paid two guineas a year for the privilege. Many of the beerhouses were run by local women, with their husbands pursuing other trades to make a living. Small establishments were therefore set up, similar to the *Queens Head*, later known as the *Drum & Monkey*, in Field Lane, Frimley, in the parlour of a timber-framed house next to the churchyard; in 1841 this was run by Elizabeth Faggetter, whose son William lived next door. It was an ideal trade for a woman who had to support herself.

In 1906, the licence for the *Drum & Monkey* was up for renewal. The beerhouse was described as being built in a country lane near to a police station, the rent was £13 a year and the house sold 3½ barrels of beer a week plus bottled beer.[21] The *Drum & Monkey* licensee was Henry Freeman who married the daughter of the previous licensee and worked as a plasterer while his wife ran the hostelry. The application to renew the licence of the beerhouse came at a time when local magistrates were trying to curb the proliferation of small premises. The application was supported by local people who probably felt more comfortable drinking in their working clothes here than in a larger inn; the occupants of 38 houses near the premises were said to use the beerhouse, as well as men employed by Rees Hall, a local farmer, and the Frimley village cricket club also relied on their supplying refreshments at matches. Despite the support of Rees Hall, at this time a local Frimley and Camberley Urban District Councillor, the licence for the *Drum & Monkey* was not renewed.

Some of the additional trades taken on by those who ran beerhouses were unrelated to inn-keeping. In Bagshot George Legge was a beerhouse-keeper and carrier of goods in 1855 and by 1878 a furniture dealer, and Henry Davis at the

87   Half Moon *beerhouse, Windlesham*

Fighting Cocks was also a carrier. Jeremiah Waddington at the *Fox & Hounds* in Yorktown was a butcher, selling beer and meat from the same premises in the 1860s, and at *The Crown* in 1874, James Street was also a plumber.[22] At the *Bird in Hand* on Jenkins Hill was the Draper family, who combined beer sales with a general shop. Other beerhouse keepers did a little farming: when the *Jolly Farmer* on the border of Bagshot and Frimley was auctioned in 1840 it had 40 acres of land attached to it;[23] and in 1849, James Boddy at the *William IV* advertised a 30-acre holding next to his establishment in the Frimley Road at Yorktown.[24] In the countryside, where trade was even slower, the additional occupations usually undertaken by beerhouse keepers were spread amongst family members. Richard Cobbett, the publican of the *Hare & Hounds* at West End, was also trading as a shoemaker, his wife Mary was making straw bonnets and they had three lodgers. Lodgers or short-stay visitors would have provided the additional basic income for many beerhouses.

The number of visitors to a beerhouse varied over time with the reputation of the hostelry and with the number of staff they employed. A variety of people passed through Bagshot on the night of the 1851 Census; guests lodging at the *Fighting Cocks* that night were a tailor 'on the tramp' from Somerset, an 18-year-old labourer from Hampshire and licensed hawker Annelly Root and his wife, who were from Holland. At *The Cricketers* were two brothers, David and John Halfacre from Blackwater, who were shoemakers probably working in Bagshot. At the *Bell and Crown* on Jenkins Hill were three labourers from Berkshire and Hampshire and a small family: Isaac Smith, a hawker from Somerset, his wife and two-month old baby, who was born in Bagshot. Lodging at a beerhouse was also a common option for local unmarried men, and at the *Travellers Rest*, later the *White Hart*, on Guildford Road in Bagshot, were three labourers, all unmarried, and all locally born.

Several attempts were made to restrict the hours that licensed premises were open, and in 1838, new hours of trade were set out in the Petty Sessions: 5am to 10pm in the summer and 6am to 10pm in winter.[25] Beerhouses were not permitted to open prior to 10am on Sundays, Good Friday and Christmas Day and there was a two-hour closure mid-afternoon from 3-5pm; these rules were regularly flouted when it was obvious that it was impossible to enforce them with just one church-appointed policeman in each village.

Owning a beerhouse was seemingly always a precarious living. In 1839, the creditors of Charles Lawrence, late licensee of the *Red Lion* at Bagshot, were invited to contact John Cave, the solicitor at Bracknell – bankruptcy being the lot of many tradesmen who had relied on visitors passing through by coach, who were now travelling by train.[26] In 1849 William Beauchamp of Burrow Hill was another publican who lost his money. His beer shop, known as *The Dolphin*, was described as a brick-and-tiled cottage with sitting rooms, kitchen, wash-house, cellar and pantry, turf house, stable, pig-sty and an excellent well when it was auctioned to pay off his debts.[27] It is likely William had converted one room in his small cottage into a beer shop, as it had the traditional right to turn out cattle and collect fuel from the heath.

It is difficult to imagine the inside of one of the beerhouses, but in July 1886 Frederick Street set out from Heatherside for an overnight trip, taking strawberries

88 Hare & Hounds *at West End*

to Covent Garden. He describes stopping off at one of these establishments in his diary:

> Our host was like the greater number of his customers rather rustic and not at all particular as to making the best of himself ... we walked into what I suppose they call the tap room but a refreshment room I called it in its truest sense, for the occupants were truly refreshing their bodies by food, drink and sleep. Around the sides of the room were rude wooden benches on which many a country carter had tried his skill at engraving figures of various shapes, and wooden stools were fixed against the wall. At one end of the room was a large open range in which was burning a brisk fire, with which the landlady was cooking and frying her eggs and bacon ... misses got us a couple of eggs apiece, two slices and a dish ah coffee, on the other side two little carter boys were sleeping soundly ... the head carter a man with four or five days growth of beard dressed with a long smock frock of a rather dirty slate colour, a round billycock hat and holding in his hand a nearly new horse whip with bright brass furls on the handle. Nearer the fire were seated another group some of which were asleep, some eating and drinking and some talking and chafing each other ... as we pushed ourselves on to one of the stools and Harry gave orders for the coffee and refreshments which we were supplied in basins and plates made of a thickness designed not to wear through by one or I might say 100 times washing and scrubbing, however we ate and drank as much as we liked and then tried to rest our spirits by a doze.[28]

BREWERS

With the number of hostelries in the area, it is not surprising that Bagshot possessed a brewery. The site of the brewery was in Brewhouse Lane, known today as Park Lane. Two kinds of beer were made in the Bagshot brewery from malt, hops, yeast and water, which were known as brown and pale malt ale. Small beer, or very weak beer, was the traditional common drink for men, women and children prior to palatable water being available. Beer would be produced which was ready for drinking within a couple of weeks, and as it did not last long, local breweries were essential. Brewing was a skilled trade and there must have been opportunities for young lads in the village to serve an apprenticeship, although no documentation has been found to confirm this. Men known to have worked as brewers include Thomas Bannister in 1764 and Thomas Tilbury who was buried in 1776, and although said to be Windlesham men, they probably worked in Bagshot. William Knight was the brewer in Bagshot in 1791 and he is believed to be of the same family as the Reading brewer Henry Knight. In 1839 James Varndell advertised as a brewer and cooper in Bagshot, his son Robert taking on the business after him. Some speculation exists that the Bagshot mill in Church Road was formerly the site of William Knight's brewery, as Manning & Bray in 1814 refer to it as 'a mill formerly a brewery'.[29]

A small brewery may also have existed at Chobham. George Percey is entered as a brewer in an 1839 local directory, and Samuel Mumford as a maltster.[30] George may have been working at one of the larger inns with a small brewery attached, and Samuel could have supplied the Bagshot brewery. It is also possible that the town-mill in Chobham was also used, in part, as a brewery.

At Frimley Green there was little passing trade, but two brewers saw the advantages of its proximity to the Basingstoke Canal, providing alternative transport to supply a wider area. The *King's Head*, which was owned by the Eversley brewer William Belsher Parfett, was built on land awarded to him in the Enclosure Act and was licensed from 1804 as a beerhouse. In the same year, the Basingstoke Canal

89 *Wharf at Frimley Green, 1870s*

Company advertised that the wharf, or unloading bay, was to be moved from the bason (probably Wharfenden Lake) to a site along the side of the canal at Frimley Green, on Belsher Parfett's land. When Belsher Parfett's estate was sold in 1854 he had dozens of public houses in the area, the coal and timber wharf at Frimley Green and a number of private houses.[31]

John Richard Birnie, a farmer and brewer, owned the *Rose & Thistle* public house, as well as Frimhurst Farm, then known as Easton Farm, both close to the canal at Frimley Green. Birnie was also Clerk to the Canal Company from 1816 until 1827, and in 1826 he became the greatest carrier on the canal with 12 barges. In 1830 Birnie carried 9,460 tons of goods, including coal and manure as well as beer and the malt used in brewing it.[32] Birnie was also established as a brewer in Basingstoke. It is not clear if another small brewery in Frimhurst Farm Cottages, known as Greenwood and Cox was owned by the brewers John Richard Birnie, William Belsher Parfett or William Cobbett, the latter being named as owning the cottages in 1842.[33]

Breweries provided extra work for barge-men in addition to their role in the movement of coal, timber and farm-produce along the waterway. In the 1841 Census, Thomas Chandler was enumerated as a barge-man moored next to the *King's Head* in Frimley Green. In 1849, Thomas Chandler's son Richard and his business partner William Haslett took over the running of the barges from Wallis & Son; their advertisement said they had formerly worked for Wallis and were offering a service from Basingstoke each Wednesday arriving in London each Saturday, and they would leave London each Friday and arrive in Basingstoke every Wednesday. The slow four-day journey from Basingstoke to London indicates how easy it would be for the railways to take the barge-men's trade.[34]

As almost all small public houses brewed their own beer, many more breweries existed in the local area. In Yorktown alone in 1851 there were brewers Henry Kinsman at *The Avenue*, Samuel Moth at the *William IV* and William Attride at the *King's Arms*.

It was not uncommon for owners of large houses and farms to have home-brewed ale where a resident or servant had the skill. Andrew Phipps of Frimley, who died 1640, left in his brew house 'one Malt querne, 4 bushells of malt with all other brewing vessels and … one bag of hopps'.[35] The contents of Frimley Park House were auctioned in 1815, and within the brew house there was 'a large stout fir bathing tub, two large working tuns, two iron-bound casks, two wooden chutes, a hop basket, a stirrer and a funnel'.[36] The poor were equally as used to brewing ale as the rich. An inventory of Chobham Workhouse in 1772 had 'in the drink room: 2 drink tubs, a kneading trough and a drink stand' plus the goods in the brew house, and in 1784 they still had a brewing copper and mashing tun.[37]

Chapter Six

TRADITIONAL VILLAGE TRADES

SHOPKEEPERS

As in all villages the butcher, baker, grocer and carpenter worked alongside the more unusual trades in the Surrey Heath area, with solicitors and bankers at the top of the scale and street vendors at the bottom. Villages in the area, other than Frimley, did not have the Manor House, church and village green format. Each village, with the exception of Windlesham, had an area where the village store was usually surrounded by other smaller businesses.

At Chobham the village was centred, as today, on the church, with a good selection of shops, and in Bagshot, the shops lined the turnpike road through the settlement. Bisley had a small shop near the village hostelry, and West End had its village shop in Brentmoor Road. The heart of Windlesham, prior to enclosure, was at Coopers Green where the village store, established in 1822 by Daniel Christmas, stood at the junction of Church Road and Kennel Lane.[1] At Frimley Green, the earliest store was situated next to the green, a site it still occupies today.

Frimley had a traditional format with the Manor House at the end of Frimley Street. Shopkeepers and tradesmen set up their businesses between the better houses in the main street, offering their wares to villagers and those passing through on this turnpike road. Another gate from the Manor House led to the village green or Grove and on to the parish church.

The development of newly-enclosed heathland settlements in the 19th century, especially Cambridge Town, Yorktown, Updown Hill and Chertsey Road in Windlesham, and eventually Lightwater, provided an opportunity for aspiring tradesmen. The new settlements brought young men, like William Ambrose Christmas, from Ockham to Yorktown, where he set up a grocery shop opposite the college. As soon as Cambridge Town developed, Christmas moved to a prime position on the corner opposite the *Cambridge Hotel* where he opened a branch of his Yorktown store and the first Post Office in the town. At Updown Hill it was Arrows Stores that employed a large number of workmen to supply the needs of the growing area of the village.

The larger villages, such as Bagshot and Chobham, were able to support more than one tradesman for each commodity. At Bagshot the bakers in 1839 were James Copas, John Frimbley, James Heathorn and the Draper family who came later;

90 *Sutton's bakery*

there was even a gingerbread maker, William Page. At Chobham, John Moir was the baker with Sutton's at Burrow Hill.[2] A similar number of butchers were also able to trade and as new opportunities arose, Webbs, who had their main shop in Bagshot, opened a second at Updown Hill in Windlesham.

A living could be made from almost every available commodity. Bottles used by brewers were collected and purchased back from men who traded in bones, rags and bottles. Charles Dillon of Bagshot advertised as a dealer in rags in 1851, or a 'rag and bone' man, who would collect, and then sell on, rags for cleaning, bones for glue and bottles to breweries. In the 1890s one man, James Legge, made a very good living as a rag dealer, employing a housekeeper and two young men as rag-sorters.

MILLERS

There were mills in every village except Bisley, most, due to the low-lying land, were water mills, but there were at least three windmills. The water mills included Town Mill and Emmetts Mill in Chobham, Windlesham Mill and Hook Mill at Windlesham and Bagshot Mill and Blackwater Mill on the northern boundary of Frimley.

91 *Staff at Arrows Store, Updown Hill, Windlesham*

WATER-MILLS

The earliest known millers at Blackwater Mill were the Chislett family. In the 1686 court records for Frimley, when Widow Chislett was living there, Blackwater Mill is described as a water mill with granary. William Chislett had died in 1666, having inherited the mill in 1608 from his father.[3] In 1746 John Ellis was the miller, and he took on Allen Mason as his apprentice. At some point between 1686 and 1791 Blackwater Mill was extended. In October 1791 the *Reading Mercury* advertised 'All those Two Water Corn Mills situate near Blackwater turnpike and usually called Blackwater Mills, which will work three pairs of stones with a convenient

92 *Christmas store, Yorktown, 1870s*

93 *Webb butchers, Updown Hill*

Millers House … The Mills, have a good-established custom.'[4] Two years later the same paper advertised that the mill had been let to George Marshall, when it was described as 'Two water Corn Mills with about Sixteen Acres of Land at Blackwater.' The estate later formed part of the purchase of land for the Royal Military College when it was valued at £1,107.[5]

Hook Mill, between Lightwater and West End, was, with its neighbour Windlesham Mill, established on behalf of Chertsey Abbey in the early 14th century.[6] Windlesham Mill was situated north-west of Hook Mill on the Windle Brook, north of Harrishaws Farm on Oldhouse Lane. Both mills were said to be owned by the Humphrey family, but at the time of the Enclosure Act of 1813, the deans and canons of Windsor were the owners of the land on which Windlesham Mill stood. In 1831, when the mill was advertised for sale, it was still a profitable concern,[7] but by the mid-19th century it was used as a saw-mill. Hook Mill on the Hale Bourne was mentioned in the perambulation of the bounds of the Godley Hundred in 1446.[8] It is likely that this was where the Thorniwork family lived and worked: Thomas in 1761 and James in 1771 were both identified as millers.[9] Hook Mill was later owned by the Humphrey family, and by 1839, Daniel Inwood was working here for them.[10] Inwood was one of several local men who took the opportunity to emigrate, and he left Windlesham for New Zealand with his wife and young family in 1850. As soon as he left, the mill was taken by James Jelley and by 1881 it was back in the hands of the Humphrey family with Hosea Humphrey working until 1895 as the miller.[11] On the O.S. map of 1898 Hook Mill it is shown as disused, and was demolished in 1899.

In Manning & Bray, Bagshot Mill was described as 'a watermill, supplied by pipes from a reservoir formed on the heath, on rising ground ... Mr Knight, who was a brewer, has quit that business, and changed his building to a mill'.[12] According to Derek Stidder, William Wright, who was a miller and also a brick maker, became bankrupt at the Bagshot Mill in 1818.[13] George Spandwick, who came from Waverley near Farnham, was a miller at Bagshot from 1832 until 1845. In 1851, when John Usher owned the mill, it was only capable of milling 25 sacks of flour a week as it had only two pairs of stones. John Rice owned the mill in 1867 when it was a steam saw-mill, as well as a corn mill; it is this later use of mills that interested men like Edwin Spooner, as every builder required a ready supply of sawn timber. In June 1882 Edwin Spooner purchased Bagshot Mill from John Rice, described as a miller and timber merchant, for £2,100. John Rice had been declared bankrupt on 24 April 1882 and his creditors had met at the *George Hotel* in Reading in May 1882. The sale of Bagshot Mill included a house, barn, saw and grist mill with engine house, mill pond, mill dam and several adjoining parcels of land.[14] In the 1940s, Mr Frank Spooner described the Bagshot Mill wheel as wooden, of 25ft in diameter and 3ft wide.[15] Later occupiers of the mill include Bagshot Saw-mills and Sunningdale Joiners. The main building was converted to flats in the late 1990s.

John Aubrey, in his *Natural History and Antiquities of Surrey*, published in 1718/9 but referring to the end of the 17th century, said there were two corn mills in the village of Chobham; it is believed that one of these was

94 *Draper family, bakers at Bagshot*

95   *Copas bakery, Bagshot*

96   *Adams' store, Frimley Green*

97   *Broomhall butchers, 1907*

98 *Boyce's delivery cart*

Emmetts Mill.[16] The name is derived from the Emmett family who lived in the village from the mid-17th century, when Richard Emmett was first mentioned in parish registers. The family is likely to have been in Chobham for generations, as according to some publications Richard Emmett was a miller in 1572. Emmetts mill was operated by Edward Jenkins in 1783, and in 1819 the mill formed part of the Ottershaw Estate when the property was auctioned. James Mumford, a farmer and miller who had occupied the mill since 1830, was the next owner, and was followed by Robert White and Robert Taylor in 1887. In the late 19th century the mill was part of an estate which included Lurking Shaw, Brimshott and Cox Hill Farms.[17]

Chobham Town Mill was erected in 1790, replacing an earlier mill established on this site by the abbot of Chertsey.[18] In the 15th century the mill formed part of the Manor of Aden.[19] For many years, Chobham Town Mill was known as Benham's mill; William Benham was born in Oakley near Basingstoke and apprenticed to Lillywhites at Nathan Mill, near his home. After his apprenticeship, Benham travelled on horseback looking for a suitable mill to purchase and start his own business and, according to his grandson Fred, he purchased the mill in the mid-19th century from Ann, the widow of James Lipscomb.[20] Benham was living and working in Chobham by 1851 and was at the mill by 1853. The only document referring to the mill prior to the Benham's ownership is one for Polores', or Brokesbourne's, property at the corner of Chertsey Road and the High Street. In the mid-17th century, the property is described as next to the course of water from the mill on the road from Guildford to Windsor.[21] The Benham family recorded that the bolting mill, *in situ* when they purchased it, had the date 1780 on it.[22] The

99 *Lightwater Post Office*

purchase of the mill was the start of an expanded business venture spanning three generations. Benham's son, Frederick Walter, took over from his father, running the mill, shop and grain-store next to their home at Florida House, now known as Frogpool House. In 1906, Frederick had a new store built on the opposite side of the High Street where he sold seed, grain, groceries and provisions, with much of the produce for the shop grown on family farms at Scotts Grove and Lovelands. Frederick Benham married the local baker's daughter, Mary Mitchell, and two of their three sons followed them into business: Frank ran the grocery counters, and Ernest the corn shop. It is Ernest that recalled the early days of the mill. In 1936, the mill wheel had been replaced by a turbine; Ernest recalled the original as 'an overshot wheel, an all metal one … the central shaft and all gear-wheels were of metal, with oak and apple cogs'. The building that housed 'the pit-wheel, the lower pivot of the central shaft, the waller, spur wheel and stone-nuts [was] boarded off, and

100 *Hook Mill, 1880s*

entered by a small door. The small room so enclosed, and rendered so dark as to need lanterns light'.[23] The original building was small, containing only two pairs of stones, therefore, William had extended it, adding a steam engine to drive two further pairs of stones. The mill closed in 1950 and was destroyed by fire in 1967. The shop and farms were sold by auction in February 1960 when the business was closed. Scotts Grove Farm and Lovelands had been sold off in the 1930s but the sale included Englefield Farm, Fowlers Wells, Florida House, Saddlers Holt, Town Mill and 15 acres of land, and realised just over £40,000.[24]

WINDMILLS

The earliest known windmill was north of the *Jolly Farmer* on the border of Bagshot and Frimley. In the Frimley Manorial records, two acres of land known as Woodley Corner are described in 1727 as that 'upon which a former windmill was erected'.[25] Only one reference to a miller in Frimley exists at an early date other than the Chislett's at Blackwater Mill, and that is of James Stevens, who died in 1658.

The second windmill in the Surrey Heath area was sited near the current *Windmill Inn* at Windlesham, built on land awarded to the Humphrey family in the 1813 Enclosure Act, with James Humphrey listed as a miller there in the 1841 and 1851 Census returns. By 1855, John Goldhawk is the licensee of the *Windmill Inn*, and as there is no further mention of a working mill it seems to have been a very short-lived venture.

101 *Town Mill, Chobham*

102 *Mill wheel, 1922*

103 *Old Mill, Frimley Green*

The third mill was sited at Guildford Road in Frimley Green, where the former structure is a feature in a house designed by architects H.R. and B.A. Poulter for Mr Frank Abbott in 1914.[26] According to the Land Tax Returns of 1784, the Guildford Road mill was owned by Mr Terry, and Thomas Lilley by 1792. In 1801 the miller was John Banks; in 1804, with the start of the building of the Royal Military College, it was purchased by the Government. A regular supply of wheat-flour would have been required at the time, and the energy generated may have been used for a saw-mill, cutting timber to build the college. The mill is not identified on the Enclosure or Tithe Maps for Frimley. In 1851 George Morgan was working the mill, probably the last man to do so.

After windmills and water mills, the third type of mill in Surrey Heath was a malt quern or mill, which was also used for grinding woad. The mill operated by using flat stones, rotated by a horse which walked around them, dragging the top stone. The malt mill was a short-term business at Buckhurst Farm in Frimley Green, where Buckhurst Road stands today. In Frimley court records, Buckhurst Farm is described as a newly-built cottage owned by Richard Gonner, in 1601.[27] The heriot due to the lord of the manor of Frimley was for a malt mill. When Richard Gonner, died his property was described as 'a cottage called Buckhurst with a malt querne and hoest … 2 bushells [of malt] all the sieves, a horse to draw the mill'. When John Stiles was admitted to this property in 1648 he had to 'take down two rooms wherein malt was dried and the other a mill house'.[28]

TANNERIES AND LEATHER WORKERS

The only known tannery site in Surrey Heath was located between Bagshot Bridge and Half Moon Street in Bagshot. In Chobham, John Wood is named as a tanner in 1588, and Richard Guye in 1622.[29] Stephen Crittenden is named in Chobham registers as a tanner in 1839, and John Gardener is a currier in the High Street in 1881.[30] With men occupied in the leather trade in Chobham, a tannery must have existed somwhere in the village. The only leather worker known to dwell in Frimley was John Davis who owned land in Frimley Green in the 1730s.[31]

A key requirement of the leather trade was the need for a constant supply of water to clean hides and immerse oak bark to make the tannin essential to 'cure' hides. The process from pelts, to a product suitable for making leather goods, took at least a year. Initially, the hide would be soaked for up to three months in vats and then laid flat in pits, with liquid tannin poured over and oak bark sandwiched between them. A mixture of warm water and animal dung was often added to the pit, until at least the end of the 19th century. A dreadful smell would have lingered near the tan-yard and, as it was situated very close to the centre of Bagshot, near to the brewery; the combination of noxious odours must have been a nuisance, especially in hot weather.

The first man named as a tanner in Bagshot was Robert Eliot in 1595.[32] Eliot died in 1596, leaving his vats to William Rawnce.[33] Later tanners include Edward Greentree in 1720, Henry Vickrey in 1764 and Joseph Child in 1773.[34] In 1801, Habakkuk Robinson purchased the business. Habakkuk was born in Bury St Edmunds in 1771, the son of Henry Robinson, a tanner. One of Habbakuk's brothers was Henry Crabb Robinson, the writer of diaries and travel journals. In his brother's

104 *A sketch of oak grinding for the tannery*

diaries, Habakkuk is referred to as 'Hab', who was in a not too successful timber business at Bagshot.[35]

In 1839, although Habakkuk was still living in Bagshot, Edmund Nicholls was the only man advertising as a tanner in the village, and he owned the tannery until 1852. In the 1891 Census, no men were listed as tanners in Surrey Heath. Tan-yard cottages, probably used to house the former workmen in Bagshot, were still standing, and Anne Allam was running a sweet shop from one of these.

LEATHER TRADESMEN

Making leather goods was a trade associated with village life for as long as records exist. Work for local farms, sales to passing trade and the ease with which leather-workers would have been able to send their finished goods to London meant that businesses flourished, especially in Bagshot. Surrey Heath men were employed as collar makers and saddlers, cordwainers and shoemakers.

Collar makers produced leather collars, harness, saddles and saddle bags. Saddle bags were required by all travellers on horseback, who utilised them for everything from a change of linen, to documents, and the 'patterns' that commercial travellers carried with them. In Chobham in 1616, John Taylor was referred to as a collar maker, and Edward Chester was a harness maker in the 1830s.[36] Henry Houlton, who had his premises almost opposite the tannery next to the *Three Mariners* in Bagshot, was one who survived in this business until the 20th century.

Cordwainers or shoemakers were essential in all villages, as shoes and boots were handmade and needed regular repairs. In Chobham, the earliest named cordwainers were Abraham Harvest in 1675 and Henry Attfield in 1758.[37] In 1839, Edward Attfield was a shoemaker at Windlesham; Charles and Edward Robinson and Thomas Rose were in Bagshot and Edward East and William Miller were in Chobham.[38] In Frimley, Thomas Thrift was a cordwainer in 1736, and Edward Elsley a shoemaker in 1743.[39]

One of the more unusual businesses using leather was established by John Wellstead, a glover in the 18th century. He and his wife had moved to Windlesham by the early 1720s. They took on at least two apprentices: John Strangwidge in 1738 and Elizabeth Fry in 1749.[40] It is not known if they sold gloves from a shop in Bagshot or sent their finished goods to London. When John died in 1798 the trade died with him. There is one other example of this trade when in 1851 at Groves Cottage in West End a man named Elijah Williams, who originated from Worcester, was enumerated as a farmer and glover.

BLACKSMITHS

The village blacksmith would not have been as busy as those attached to the military or those along the road to London. Some, like Christopher Graunt who died in 1582 in Windlesham, had additional trades.[41] Graunt was a smallholder, leaving a number of sheep to members of his family. Many blacksmiths had yards next to wheelwrights.

105   *The Bourne, a source of water for the tannery, Bagshot*

Each village in the Surrey Heath area had blacksmiths with, as would be expected, a larger number in Bagshot and Chobham. Frimley, a relatively small settlement at the time, supported two: John Cox in 1631 and John Sewell in 1632, who were likely to have been engaged in general farriery work, making and mending carts and farm machinery or repairing metal household goods; they would also have made windows and a variety of hinges for house builders.[42] Edward Ryde, the surveyor, wrote in his diary in 1844 that when the adjusting screws on his theodolite failed he took it to a Chobham blacksmith to be repaired.[43]

Families specialised in the blacksmith trade, handing down skills through the generations. The Mose family were one example; they had forges at Chobham, West End and in 1851 at Pound Cottage in Bisley. The Street family at Chobham had two premises in the village with George and James working in 1839.[44] At Frimley, Thomas Thrift is named as a blacksmith who was assigned property in 1715.[45] This was on the south side of Frimley Street, a site known to have an operating forge until just before it was demolished in the 1960s. After Thomas Thrift's death, it is not clear who worked here until the arrival of the Wynn family in 1796, who had been farriers in Windlesham. John and William Wynn also made clocks, of which there are two examples in Surrey Heath Museum, and one in an American museum. The Wynn family continued as blacksmiths in the village until the early 20th century when George Kinchen came to the village. George, who was born in Hartley Wintney, moved to Frimley in the mid-1880s to work for William Wynn. George Kinchen's sons took over from him and the forge stayed in his family until it was demolished.

106 *Houlton, collar-maker at Bagshot*

107 *Windlesham Forge*

In Bagshot, the Hayter family worked as smiths. In 1778, Charles Hayter was a witness in a case of theft when a watchmaker from Staines absconded with property belonging to a former employer and sold it to Charles. In any small village it was important to be seen as honest, and Charles was no exception:

> The prisoner had taken a shop near me; he came to me with these locks, and said, he had formerly dealt in these things, but wanted money … hearing afterwards there was a search-warrant in his house. And fearing that these things might be stolen, I went and informed the prosecutor.[46]

Samuel Hayter, the nephew of Charles, continued to trade in Bagshot until the early 19th century, but this was a family which suffered from the decline in the carriage trade. Samuel's widow tried to continue after his death, but in September 1839 her case for insolvency was heard when:

> An elderly female named Hayter applied to be discharged. It appeared that she had been a smith and farrier at Bagshot and ascribed her insolvency to the railways. Her son stated that forty-five coaches used to pass through the town, which brought considerable business to his mother, but at this time there were only four, the others having been taken off on account of the railways.[47]

As some said the blacksmith trade was dying, others moved in to Bagshot to pursue it. Benjamin Cudlipp, born in Bursledon in Hampshire in 1832, moved to Hawley by 1865 with his small family, and to Bagshot by 1867 where he saw an opening for trade, as there was only one other blacksmith, William Evans.[48] William Evans traded as a farrier and ironmonger, and when he died in 1870, he was succeeded by his son Stephen, who continued as an ironmonger and who also became the village postmaster.

108   *Sketch of Wynn clock*

At Burrow Hill in Chobham and in Frimley Road in Camberley there were examples of the use of adjoining premises as blacksmiths shops and beerhouses; both were named the *Four Horse Shoes*, and both licensed premises still bear the name today. George Hurdle was the first to open a beer shop and smithy in Frimley Road, and by 1889 James Horrocks, late Sergeant-Farrier of the 5th Dragoon Guards, was advertising as a blacksmith and farrier here.[49] Horrocks was also listed as the licensee of the public house from 1886 until 1891 – it is not clear when the businesses ceased to be a smithy.

At Burrow Hill it is uncertain when the beerhouse opened. Mr Crawley, the licensee in 1957, described the business then as a beerhouse, which had operated for over 250 years. 'Prior to that the building was the village smithy. There was just one light over a small hatch from which the beer was served, a room that was seldom open, and a darts room.'[50] The smithy trade was flourishing in the mid-19th century at Burrow Hill; there was a cluster of men working near the green which included William Terry and William Boylett. A small building exists today, near the public house that was a smithy in more recent times.

109 *Burrow Hill at Chobham*

The old smithy owned by the Mose family at Coldharbour in West End continued to trade, and as the village expanded, a new forge opened in Guildford Road. The forge was set up in the 1880s by Herbert Gosden when he purchased a third of an acre of land on the corner of High Street and Guildford Road. When Herbert died in 1939, his son Ben took over and offered a service as a wheelwright as well as a smith. As the horse-trade declined, Ben's two sons John and Bob operated as general smiths and engineers, taking orders for arrow heads, swords, and medieval helmets for enthusiasts re-enacting battles. The sons also made the village sign, prior to their retirement in 1994.[51] Today, there are no traditional blacksmiths or their forges left in Surrey Heath, even though much of the land traditionally used for farming has been turned into paddocks for horses.

WHEELWRIGHTS

Considered an important trade in any village, wheelwrights made and repaired carts and general wooden goods. Due to the turnpike roads passing through Surrey Heath, there would have been a passing trade in addition to village needs for wheelwrights. George Sturt of Farnham pointed out in his book, *The Wheelwright's Shop*, that each customer had very exacting requirements for their carts, depending on the width of ruts in lanes leading to his property, the slope of the land and the tradition of style and shape they had used for generations. [52]

Some wheelwrights are named in apprenticeship or removal documents: John Sleet of Chobham was sent back to his village from West Drayton in 1723; Robert Bedborough of Chobham and William Ellis of Windlesham were both named in apprenticeship records in the 18th century: Henry Street was named at Windlesham in 1752, with a further Henry there in 1831; Alfred and James Carpenter were in Chobham in 1851; James, John and Peter Kent were in Yorktown and George and

110   *Mose Forge, West End*

Thomas Ridgers were at Bagshot. Wheelwrights worked using many of the same tools and materials as carpenters, and some men worked as both. John Soane in 1851 is described as a wheeler and carpenter in Frimley Green at a site just off Guildford Road.

Very few locations have been clearly identified as the sites of wheelwrights' shops, although their general position is known. In Frimley in 1842 there was a shop run by Moses Finch on the Grove, and John Wooldridge was working at a site near Mytchett Bridge on the Basingstoke Canal. Peter Kent was on Osnaburgh Hill in Yorktown; in 1813 Henry Street was in Guildford Road, Lightwater, probably the site used in 1851 by James Trigg; William Rapley in 1851 worked in Chertsey Road, Windlesham, with Thomas Ridgers in Updown Hill and William Hall in Church Road. Another Thomas Ridgers and his son George was on Jenkins Hill in Bagshot, and in Chobham James Carpenter worked in Burrow Hill, next to the blacksmith. One of the sites believed to have been a wheelwright's shop was along the eastern edge of the Bourne near Bagshot Bridge; a document relating to adjoining property in 1859 refers to 'All that smiths shop, carpenters shop and sawpit ... bound on one side by the River Bourne there and then in the occ of William Ede, blacksmith and farrier'.[53] The wheelwrights' trade probably suffered in the village as the coach trade declined.

The types of goods produced by a local wheelwright were as diverse as their customers. John and George Parker, who worked in Darby Green just over the boundary from Surrey Heath, listed every item made and the full name, age and date of death of those they made coffins for.[54] In the 1840s, the greatest sum of money was charged for building, converting or repairing carts, but the family also adapted items, as in 1843 when John Parker made a razor-grinding barrow for Mr Dean and a 'bung-hole to cart and fixing a coffee mill for Mr Prior'. Chairs and tables, bedroom floors and house roofs, fowl coops, pig troughs, salting troughs, ladders and pumps were all repaired. Turf irons were re-handled, new rims were provided for wheels and handsaws sharpened. The Parker's made packing cases, coffins, cow cribs, harrows and rakes, wheelbarrows, pig troughs of numerous sizes and hay racks, and for the householder they made furniture, night commodes, copper lids, ash boxes, bee stools and bee blocks, oven peels and lids, washing stools and ironing boards. The brothers also made tools for other workmen including forge rims or curbs for Robert Wynn, the blacksmith. Mr Forder, who was probably a publican, ordered a set of skittles and they made and fixed a skittle frame for him. The brothers even made a cricket bat. John and George Parker seem to have had a set price for all tasks, perhaps charging slightly more if the client was just passing through. In 1844 the brothers charged 10s. for four days' work, or 2s. 6d. a day plus materials; not a lot more than a labourer would have earned at this time.

COACHBUILDERS

Traditionally, coachbuilders used their skills alongside the wheelwrights and blacksmith, and as fewer carriages were made they turned their skills to making hoods for motorised vehicles. It is not until the late 19th century, with the decline of the trade in many towns, that coachbuilders are identified in Surrey Heath.

The Attewell family arrived in 1879, when Albert Attewell lived near the *Railway Arms* in Frimley High Street.[55] In the 1890s, the family were living in

111 *Len and Frank Warr ringing a wheel*

112   *Mr Kearley, wheelwright at Frimley Green*

Frimley Road, a site eventually owned by Whites garage. In 1891, Albert and his eldest son were coachbuilders, and two younger sons were apprenticed to him. In 1896 Albert applied to have a new workshop built on the site.[56] Albert died prior to 1900 and his seven sons, all of whom had received training in an aspect of the coach-building trade, could not agree how to run the business and by 1901 it was sold to Ernest Field.[57] Field traded as Camberley Carriage Works in partnership with Mr Sharpe, and in 1906 they extended the business by adding another workshop at the site and purchasing Wokingham saw-mill. In *Yorktown Parish Magazine* in 1909 Ernest D. Field wished to inform 'the Nobility and Gentry of the district' that they had purchased Lunn Brothers Motor Works and Cycle business, a long-standing Yorktown business, situated opposite the junction of Laundry Lane and the London Road. The business had previously been an ironmongers founded by John Lunn in the early 1870s, which was taken over by his sons Henry and Augustus in the 1880s.

After the First World War, Ernest Field's younger brother Frederick advertised in the *Camberley News* that he had served for three years in the Royal Army Service Corps Mechanical Transport section. The half-page advertisement, which included a photograph of the business premises (a novelty at this time), stated that the business were builders of motor bodies and hoods for carts and carriages.[58] Later the same year, the Field's business was purchased by the Slope family, who had large ambitions for the site; they manufactured bodies for buses and charabancs, employing almost forty men. The Slope family had been awarded a contract to build bodies for 12 buses for Guernsey Motors at £133 10s. per carriage, undercutting the only other quote of £178 10s.[59] An additional workshop was built by Slopes in April 1920. The Guernsey Motors contract seems to have been unprofitable, and after the first six bodies had been made the Slope family were writing to ask for more money for the remainder, as they had lost money on those delivered; they received an extra £50 per carriage and delivered three more, but then it seems they were unable to trade and by the spring of 1922 were selling off the contents of the workshops. Later that year the site was purchased by Percy White whose company retained it until the late 20th century.

Businesses that survived were those that adapted to mechanical, rather than carpentry-based skills, as the motor car took precedence. Among the the adaptable businesses and businessmen was James Boorman, who arrived in Yorktown as a young man in the 1870s, when he was already described as a 'master coachbuilder' although he was just 28 years old.[60] Boorman's business, which was situated opposite the Yorktown entrance to the R.M.C., offered to store carriages, to let them on hire or make any style of carriage.[61] The business was conveniently situated next door to the smithy run by the Traviss family, and in 1901 Boorman applied to have a new smithy built. Trading as J. Boorman and Son in 1914, he no longer advertised as a carriage builder but sold Humber, Singer and Triumph cars and Singer motor cycles from his 'Well equipped Garage with Electric Light'.[62]

113 *Attewell's yard, Frimley Road, 1890s*

114   *Two views of Camberley Carriage Works*

SAWYERS

The trade of a sawyer is ancient, but it is only from the 19th century that it appears in local records as a separate or identifiable trade, perhaps due to the planting of thousands of acres of fir trees, post-enclosure. Sawyers certainly gained a reputation for hard work and were well remembered locally, as:

> They needed to be strong for their craft was exceptionally tiring, demanding not only skill but brute strength as well … and at the same time they had to be judges of the wood, of all its virtues and defects. Their craft came between that of the woodman … and the carpenter and wheelwright who made use of the sawyer's art. They knew and appreciated the special needs of both latter craftsmen, how to cut for the carpenter an oak log four feet in diameter into planks of no more than one inch thickness, how to cut for the wheelwright the many parts that went to make up a wagon.[63]

In 1841 in Bagshot, Luke Baker, his sons Luke and William, and William Brant were sawyers. It was a flourishing trade and 10 years later James Cooper, George, James and John Parker of Frimley, Arthur, Charles and Joshua Ottaway in Chobham, George Bernard and Alfred and John Jones of Bagshot, William Oliver in Bisley and John Baker in Windlesham all worked as sawyers.

A number of sawyers took the opportunity to emigrate as they were in great demand in the new world. After the Treaty of Waitangu in 1840, New Zealand became a colony of Britain and men were encouraged to emigrate by being offered a free passage. Edward Baigent, the second son of Thomas and Dorothy of Windlesham, was one of the first men who took the opportunity; he sailed on the *Clifford* arriving in New Zealand on 11 May 1842, with his wife Mary Ann and five children. The family travelled with David and Elizabeth Clark and their children who were also from Bagshot, and leased land in Brook Street Valley, where both

115 *Bagshot saw-mill, 1919*

116 *Windlesham Military Hospital, First World War*

families erected Maori-type dwellings.[64] Shortly after, due to a shortage of money, Edward went to find work in Wakefield, a settlement on the Waimea River; he eventually became the largest landowner in the Waimea South area, leasing a native forest block in 1843 and setting up a small water mill in 1844 with materials he had brought from Windlesham. Baigent's water mill was used as a timber saw-mill during the day and a flour mill at night – 'By the 1880s Baigent's Wakefield mill was producing one sixth of the province's output'.[65] Edward's son Lewis saw the advantages of growing a sustainable pine tree crop in New Zealand, and the Baigent name continues today in one of the major timber businesses in that region of the country with a share of the 2,060-acre forest. Edward was followed a few years later by his brother Isaac and his wife Jane. Although the Baigents were the main family with this trade to emigrate, there were others from Surrey Heath, including William Brant, who married Mary Gale in Windlesham in 1841; they emigrated soon after their marriage, predating the emigration of the Baigents and the Clarkes, and were the first local people known to have opted to emigrate to New Zealand, but where they settled and how they prospered is unknown.

Saw-Mills

Saw-mills were established in most Surrey Heath villages by the late 19th century, especially as by then they could be driven by steam. As soon as development of Cambridge Town started in 1862, a steam saw-mill was erected in Park Street. In 1867 Augustus and Thomas Winter were advertising as contractors, timber and slate merchants, steam flour and saw-millers, but the Park Street mill had gone by 1889.[66]

Extensive plantations on the Bagshot Park estate were looked after by Crown Woodsman. In 1891, Richard Wye held the position living in the newly built Post Office at Jolly Farmer Hill where his wife was the postmistress. The Bagshot Park plantations, though less extensive by the First World War, proved a valuable asset when the war made for greater difficulty in obtaining timber from abroad. The Canadian Timber Corps was utilised, setting up a logging operation and a saw-mill near Rapley Lake in Bagshot, and pine from here was sent all over Britain for use in mines and for fencing. Windlesham Military Hospital was well used by members of the Timber Corps, as many of the men sustained injuries nearby at the mill.[67] Not all Timber Corps casualties were due to the work however; the inquest on Samuel Hunter of the Corps found that he lay on the ground intoxicated and was run over by a vehicle.[68]

Local Scots pine trees were also tapped for turpentine, another commodity in short supply.[69] In both World Wars there was a shortage of materials, especially wood for the building industry. With the start of the Second World War in 1939, Montague L. Meyer acquired part of the woodland near Hammond Pond, now in Lightwater Country Park, where they set up a saw-mill to provide timber for the building industry.

Plots of land in Surrey Heath continued to be planted with fir rather than deciduous trees until the development of the area after the Second World War, when the value of land increased as housing estates were built. Experimental plots of fir plantations existed on Old Dean Common in 1957 and the Forestry Commission were concerned that this 70-year-old woodland with five sample plots was to be cleared to make way for housing. The experimental work of the Forestry Commission at this time included light and heavy thinning on the volume production of Scots pine; they hoped that the Council could be persuaded to leave this land for as long as possible to allow them to continue the work. However, the pressure for houses was considered to be more important.[70]

117   *Burrows builders yard, Chobham*

BUILDERS AND CARPENTERS

The history of the building trade in Surrey Heath follows the pattern of most village trades until the beginning of the 19th century and the erection of the Royal Military College at Sandhurst. Prior to 1800, each of the local villages would have had their own carpenter and joiner; the larger villages of Chobham and Bagshot had bricklayers, who also did a little plastering.

Individual men capable of building a property are only identifiable when they appear in parish records, as when Moses Beauchamp was contracted to build a new workhouse in Chobham in 1790, and Mark Stevenson was paid £1 18s. for digging a new well.[71] In the mid-19th century, one or two general builders are mentioned in the Census returns: William Allbery, a retired builder in 1851, and Henry Faggeter, described as a Master Builder, both of whom were living in Frimley; and Jeremiah Howard, a carpenter and builder of Chobham. There were also painters and glaziers: William Ellis in Bagshot and Alfred Stevens in Chobham; and plumbers and glaziers William Smithers in Bagshot and Edward Stevens and Ephraim Bragg in Chobham. At a later date, incomers Edwin Spooner in Bagshot and Thomas Dale at Windlesham established businesses employing large numbers of local men.

The development of Yorktown and Cambridge Town attracted ambitious tradesmen, initially to work on building the colleges. The land on the south of the turnpike road opposite the colleges was owned by two men anxious to sell it on: Captain Charles Raleigh Knight and his brother-in-law Major Spring who owned almost all the land between Portsmouth Road and the London Road from the *Jolly Farmer* to Blackwater Bridge. The Staff College, which was completed in 1862, gave Captain Knight an opportunity to lay out a new town on a grid pattern, with housing for the working classes lining the streets nearest the college. The men who worked on Captain Knight's development were not 'home-grown' as formerly seen in the villages of Surrey Heath, but men with aspirations to establish their own small business or to become a developer.

Opportunities were arising for all aspects of the building trade, including architects, developers and estate agents, many of whom moved up from the West Country, especially Dorset, having made money from the development of towns such as Bournemouth. Other workers were apprenticed in Devon, Dorset, or even Suffolk and Norfolk, and moved to the Surrey Heath area as single, ambitious young men. New developments included shops interspaced with housing and pubs, stretching almost from Blackwater Bridge to the newly-built *Cambridge Hotel* opposite the Royal Military and Staff Colleges. It was the trade from these army colleges that created a multitude of opportunities for energetic and ambitious shopkeepers, publicans and tradesmen who had moved to the area.[72]

One example of the men who came and stayed in the area was Alfred Tanner, born in Colerne in Wiltshire in 1841, who came to Yorktown in 1860 to work on the building of the Staff College and the wings to the Royal Military College and Broadmoor, and subsequently set up his own business as a carpenter and undertaker.[73] Tanner's work was carried on by his son, also Alfred, on a site on Osnaburgh Hill. After Alfred died in 1919, his son had a sweet shop and tobacconist operating in conjunction with his trade as an undertaker, and his family still live in the town today.

Chapter Seven

Nursery Work

Bagshot, Sunningdale and Windlesham Nurseries

The plant-nursery industry became the largest single source of employment in Surrey Heath, after the army. The land used for the plant nurseries became a new vibrant landscape with sweet-smelling shrubs and plants. A formerly rather drab, somewhat monotonous and sparse landscape now included areas densely packed with colourful plants, providing inspiration for landholders wishing to landscape the grounds of their new estates.

After the enclosure of the heathland, the bulk of allotments in Windlesham and Bagshot were improved for use as nursery land, a medium entirely suited to new plants being introduced in the early 19th century by plant hunters. John Taylor, the only man in Surrey Heath known to have earned a living as a nurseryman pre-enclosure, had established his nursery in Bagshot by 1791 when he had converted part of the peat moor at the western end of the village into a nursery-ground.[1] In addition, John Taylor also owned 4½ acres near Bagshot Green and rented a further quarter of an acre.[2] In all, less than five acres of traditional farmland in the whole of Surrey Heath at the end of the 18th century were used as nursery land. An early description of Taylor's nursery stated that 'he sells all his plants when they are young, for the bottom is gravel and will not allow them to stand long'.[3] He received 45 acres in the Enclosure Award of 1812, and also rented additional fields next to the workhouse, which stood near the Almshouses on Guildford Road. John Taylor also owned five cottages, and it is likely some of the men occupying these were his employees, whom in 1811 included John Langford, John Clark, George Elliott, Samuel Crampton and Richard Carey.[4] John Taylor died in June 1828 and left his estate to his second wife Susannah, who sold the nursery to Michael Waterer in 1829 for the sum of £1,665; it was not the earliest of the Waterer's nurseries, but it is the first they owned in Surrey Heath.

John Waterer was a smallholder of Ryde Heron in Knaphill, and the first nurseryman in the family. When John died in 1780, he left the nursery to his nephew Michael who died in 1827, and his eldest son of the same name inherited. Michael Waterer junior purchased John Taylor's business in 1829 and at this time it consisted of land to the north of Jenkins Hill. Michael had two younger brothers: John, who ran the Bagshot nursery, and Hosea, who did the same at

119

Knaphill.[5] Michael died from cholera in 1842, and his brothers inherited the estate, but could not agree to run the business jointly. Hosea took the Knaphill business and John the Bagshot site, and both advertised in *The Gardener's Chronicle* of 16 November 1844 that from this date, the businesses would be run separately. The stock at Bagshot in 1844 included 6,000 Spanish chestnuts, 50,000 larch firs, 50,000 birch and John's 'unrivalled' stock of cedars. In *The Gardener's Chronicle* in 1848 the Bagshot nursery was described as 30 acres of fine peaty soil divided by hedges into square compartments containing dense shrubberies. The boxed off compartments were created to provide the greatest spectacle as the plants came in to flower; rhododendrons, azaleas, kalmias, laurel and lilac were grown, which prospective purchasers were encouraged to come and view. Nurseries relied on visitors, most of whom would arrive at the nearest railway station, and employment was found for numerous carriers and carters transporting people and plants to and from the sites.

Waterer's Bagshot nursery employed dozens of men, some women (seasonally) and a few boys. In 1867 John's extended nursery was examined by a commissioner, enquiring into the employment of women and children. John told them his nursery was:

> About 120 acres in extent. We employ four or five women in summer, but not regularly; their principal work is weeding and cleaning the ground. They earn about 1/- a day and work from 8 or 9am until 5pm. We don't employ young girls. We employ four or five boys aged from 9 to 12, they are employed constantly; they wait on the men. We employ 40 men all the year round and at times as many as 60 to 70. We employ the boys because they come and ask for work; their labour is not of great importance to us; we pay them 4/- to 8/- a week. The other nursery gardeners about here employ labour in the same way as we do.[6]

His son John Waterer became one of the most successful nurserymen with a branch office in Philadelphia. With an income reputed to be £10,000 a year by the turn of the century, John Waterer was also responsible for producing the best known rhododendron of the era, Pink Pearl. The time of great expansion in the nursery trade was from 1871 until the time of John's death in 1893. By the beginning of the 20th century, the Waterer company was in financial difficulties. In 1914, the Bagshot nursery amalgamated with the Wargrave Plant Farm of Twyford and became known as John Waterer, Sons and Crisp. The importance of the American market to the Waterer nurseries is clear, as Gomer, John's son, made more than twenty trips there between 1893 and 1917 to obtain orders.

Although Waterer's is the longest established of all the nurseries in Surrey Heath, Sunningdale Nursery, owned by Charles Noble and John Standish, established in 1847, became the most influential. John Standish had worked as a gardener at Bagshot Park under Andrew Toward prior to setting up his Royal or Dukes Hill Nursery *c.*1840 on land virtually adjoining Bagshot Park. When Charles Noble joined Standish in 1846, he retained the nursery site and they opened a second and larger nursery along the London Road, nearer to Sunningdale Station.[7] From 1849, the plant hunter Sir Joseph Hooker sent Noble and Standish rhododendron seeds and cuttings from Sikkim, which they propagated, providing a stock of plants which were eventually moved to Castle Howard in Yorkshire by James Russell in 1968, and which formed the basis for a collection which is now one of very few sources of the earliest of these stock plants in the country. Standish and Noble also sponsored Robert Fortune in one of his expeditions to Japan and by 1849 they were selling plants he had collected. John Standish left the partnership in 1856, but Charles Noble continued to run the business until he retired in 1896.

One of the young apprentices that Noble took on was Harry White, who started work in 1867. Harry managed the business, and after Noble's death he continued running it for the new owners, initially the Kemp-Welch family and later Sir Hubert Longman.[8] White was an expert in the cultivation of rhododendrons and it was due to his care of the original stock that they survived the First World War, when he was down to just a couple of elderly men helping him to run the site. Individuals that purchased plants from him included Edward, Prince of Wales, and in 1918, Major Lionel Rothschild, who bought azaleas and rhododendrons for his Exbury Estate. Harry White died in 1936, and in 1939 the nursery was purchased by N. Hamilton-Smith and Major Herbert Russell, with Louis Gray as the manager.[9] After the Second World War, the nursery gained a reputation for being the most beautiful nursery in the country, it was a place where visitors arrived at the weekend and viewed the long borders and shrubberies, admiring the excellent stock growing there. Those responsible for the reputation of the nursery were James Russell, an expert in the cultivation of rhododendrons, and, after 1956, Graham Stuart Thomas, whose knowledge of roses was renowned. When the nursery was sold to John Waterer, Sons and Crisp in 1968, the best of the azaleas and rhododendrons were moved, to become the National Collection at Castle Howard, and the roses went to the Royal National Rose Collections at St Alban's and Mottisfont.

This land adjoining the London Road between Bagshot and Sunningdale is still the prime area for nurseries. Other early nursery businesses along this road included Lavershot, or the American Nursery, established by Richard Dare before 1820, and purchased by the Hammond family. Just off the main London Road in Hatton Hill was Aaron Mason's nursery, which was established prior to 1851, and in the 1870s, his son Richard was running it. When Richard died in 1893 the nursery was put up for sale, and eventually, in 1899, part of his land was sold to Fromow's.[10]

William Fromow founded Fromow's nursery in 1829 at Chiswick. In the 1881 Census, Fromow's son William was employing 20 men as well as his four sons, James Jabez, Joseph, Edwin and William, and the Nursery was known as Fromow and Sons. Although operating in London, the Fromow family were well aware of local nurseries, purchasing plants annually from Heatherside as well as occasional orders from Sunningdale. The Fromow family purchased Astage Hill farmhouse in Windlesham at auction in 1893. With land formerly of Aaron Mason's in Hatton Hill, they had the benefit of a variety of soil conditions. After the death of James Jabez, William junior, Edwin, Joseph, and his two sons, Cecil and Alfred, took over the Windlesham nursery.[11] Although many members of the family were involved in the running of Fromow's, much of its success was due to the employment of

118   *Waterer's horse and cart loaded with heather and fern, Chobham*

the nursery manager, William Richard Oldham, who initially worked for the family at Chiswick and came to Windlesham in 1897 when the nursery covered just 30 acres of land.[12] Oldham became very involved in the running of the village and was elected to the Parish Council 16 months after he arrived, and after 32 years in local affairs, eventually as Chairman of the Windlesham Urban District Council, he retired from service in 1928. Oldham was also a school manager and Guardian of the Poor, and set up a charity during the First World War collecting funds for families in need. All this work in the village was in addition to his professional life as a member of the Council of the Royal Horticultural Society and President of the Horticultural Trades Association.

During the late 19th and early 20th centuries, numerous men from Windlesham and Lightwater worked for Fromow's, which specialised in growing trees, shrubs and rhododendrons; they were also able to raise fruit trees and roses on the clay soil of Astage Hill Farm. Initially, men from Bagshot and Windlesham were employed, but gradually the area around the western edge of the land was used for building housing suitable for the 'labouring classes'; houses in Guildford Road, at Lightwater, and similar housing on the roads leading from it, were ideal for men who had limited funds to rent a property. Gradually, the village of Lightwater expanded, fuelled by the convenient source of employment from Fromow's. Shops and facilities were established on what had been a rather empty and desolate portion of heathland between Bagshot and West End, with just a few traditional farms to the east of the

Guildford Road. Lightwater became a thriving community, which in turn provided extra employment for builders, other small nurserymen and small-scale poultry farmers. In the 1960s, there were just 11 men working on the South Farm part of Fromow's, plus part-timers and students in the summer, five worked at Astage Hill Farm full time and another five in the Home Nursery, with a further two or three employed in the glass houses.[13] Many trees which became established on the Fromow's nursery ground form part of the extensive local arboretum currently owned by a Trust set up by Major Spowers.

Russell's Nursery was established by John Russell in London in 1840 and eventually expanded to a site near the Lords Cricket Ground, a usage still referred to today when cricket commentators mention the 'nursery end' of this famous sports ground. Russell's business expanded, with sites in Richmond in 1902 and others around the south of the country. During the First World War, Russell was unable to continue running this extensive empire due to shortage of manpower, and it was all sold off apart from the Richmond site. In 1935, in an effort to expand the business, Louis Russell purchased a site at Windlesham, which had been Richard Dare's Lavershot Nursery; it was established as L.R. Russell, and after the Second World War was sometimes confused with James Russell's nursery, which was on adjoining land. Another two generations of the Russell family traded from the Windlesham site, as John Russell took over from his father Louis, and his son Louis Robert Russell followed him, and in 1958 they were one of the first local nurserymen to open a garden centre.[14]

Today, a line of garden centres still exist along the London Road from Notcutts in Bagshot to almost Sunningdale Station.

119   *Rhododendron walk at Waterer's nursery*

120 *Waterer's canned roses*

CAMBERLEY AND FRIMLEY NURSERIES

In the northern strip of the Manor of Frimley (Camberley today) at least two plant nurseries were established post-enclosure, the earliest was on a plot of land now used as the Recreation Ground in London Road, with its Nursery House approximately where the Arena Leisure Centre now stands. It is believed that John Tough, a nurseryman from Bradford Peverell in Dorset, purchased 12 acres of land from John Tekell in 1812 for a sum of £960, although it was likely that he leased the land from John Tekell prior to this date.[15] The nursery was left to Tough's eldest son in 1813, and when his son died the following September, the nursery was put up for sale in November 1815. At the time the Tithe Map was produced in 1842 the land is referred to as 'late John Tough's Nursery'.

The second and more long-lasting of the two plant nurseries was established by John Craig at Barossa Farm, north of the centre of Camberley. Craig started his working life in Scotland, arriving in England by 1851, where he became head gardener to Sir Joseph Paxton, the famous landscape designer who laid out the grounds at Crystal Palace. Craig moved to Bagshot Park in the late 1850s and worked with John Standish.[16] John Craig purchased Barossa Farm in Camberley in 1861, erected large glasshouses and named his business The Nursery Grounds. In 1862 he laid out the parkland surrounding Frimley Park House for its new owner William Crompton Stansfield and was responsible for laying out the grounds around the Queen's Pavilion at Aldershot and Wellington College.[17] Craig's son Wallace continued in the family tradition, setting up a shop at the top of Camberley High Street, where in *Drew's Directory* for 1914 he was a florist, seeds man and horticultural sundries man with a nursery ground in Gordon Road.

The largest of the Frimley nurseries was Heatherside. It is thought that Heatherside's founder, Augustus Mongredien, was born in London in 1806 and was the son of Adrien Mongredien who migrated to England from France in 1802. The family came from Saint Nicolas D'Attez and it is said they left France due to their royalist origins. Mongredien wrote on such diverse topics as free trade and botany; he was also a leading chess master. Some of the publications and pamphlets known to have been written by Mongredien are *Trees and Shrubs for English Plantations* in 1870 and *Heatherside Manual of Trees and Shrubs* in 1874/5.

By 1871 Heatherside nursery was laid out with avenues of trees with an 'English garden' surrounding the main house, and prospective purchasers of Mongredien's stock were invited to stroll through the grounds where fountains and statues adorned the site. One of the reasons Augustus Mongredien may have chosen the site at Heatherside for a nursery is explained in his book: 'Experience has shown that tender plants are more liable to casualties when grown in damp or sheltered valleys than when cultivated in high and more exposed situations … as the growth is commenced later and ceases sooner, so as to allow the wood to ripen.'[18]

Some evidence exists to support a long-held belief that Augustus Mongredien grew *Ailanthus glandulosa* at Heatherside, where on part of his nursery he established a silk farm. It is certain that examples of Ailanthus were grown at Heatherside and it is likely that Mongredien attempted an experiment here, as he freely admits in his book that 'The Bombyx Cynthia, a species of silk-worm feeds on its leaves … attempts have been made to rear it in England on a large scale. Hitherto, however, the experiment has proved unsuccessful.'[19] Mongredien went on to say that 'Had the Ailantus done what was expected of it – supplied the abundance of leaves for food – it is possible that the cocoons … low-priced as they were, might have yielded enough to pay a fair rent per acre on poor soils.' As Mongredien also owned land in the West Country and in Kent the experiment could have been held at any of his properties, although given the statement about the use of poor soil it would quite likely have been Heatherside.

In 1873, the Heatherside Nursery Company was formed, offering shares at £10 each in an attempt to re-finance the business as it had not been a financial success. In 1865, Mongredien had employed a local smallholder and nurseryman, Frederick Street of Fellow Green, West End, to plant an avenue of Wellingtonia trees; it was one of several avenues planted to provide a wind- and frost-break for more delicate plants in the nursery grounds. It is said Frederick Street was not paid for his work and when The Heatherside Nursery Company was bankrupt in 1875, their bankers, the Golney family, took over the estate and he was appointed nursery manager.[20]

121   *Sir Joseph Hooker*

It appears that after Frederick Street's arrival at Heatherside, a farm was established within the grounds of the nursery. Frederick Street and his family lived in Nursery Cottage, an amalgamation of two of the four cottages that stand near the junction of Upper Chobham Road and the Maultway. Born in Bisley, Street had increased the productivity of his West End smallholding by utilising a portion of it as nursery land, and with his farming and horticultural skills, he was able to manage a dairy farm and a successful nursery at Heatherside for the Goldney family, as well as overseeing the letting of Heatherside House. Street's work was varied, with much of it entailing travelling, and would have been more difficult without assistance from his eldest son Frederick, who took on much of the bookkeeping, invoicing and running of the nursery. Frederick junior also kept a diary in which he recorded daily life at Heatherside; the entries provide insight into the work carried out, the pressure of providing clients with the quality of work anticipated, and the men that worked with them. References to daily life within a nursery and farm, illustrated in Frederick's diary, give insights into how men were employed, the relationship with clients and the owners the Goldney's, and how exasperating it could be to work this difficult land:

5th February 1886 – Spent most of our time at Colonel Maurice [Highland View] and planting a belt of trees at Camberley for a Mr Doman also we have taken some work from Mrs Fenwick at Meopham House where we have started four men at work. It is now very hard for Father who is with the men in the day and till 10 or 11 at night at correspondence and books. We have this week commenced making a tennis lawn an orchard, trenching a course, planting a belt and a hedge for Colonel Maurice employing some 16 men there.[21]

The work at Heatherside was varied but constant:

March 1889 – making a tennis lawn for Mr Stone at Ravenswood … on the 16th and 18th we had a very grand ball room to decorate on the occasion of the marriage of Mrs Ferguson's daughter to Mr Harris at Yorktown, it was an exceedingly well managed affair and took the greater part of our flowering plants besides a large number of shrubs potted to decorate it.

Greenhouse work at Heatherside included grafting rhododendrons and clematis, where almost 4,000 plants were being raised. Extra land at the nursery was cleared for rhododendrons to be planted out, and 'On the farm we are now preparing all the Cedar Valley for laying down to permanent pasture, and the Beech and Oak Valley Fields for potatoes.' Many of the rhododendrons planted were not propagated, but bought in, for example, in May 1887 the Street's purchased 6,000 plants from a sale at Milford.

Frederick Street junior's diary also provides a view of the conditions under which men were employed: 'Saturday 19th June 1886. We have tonight discharged a number of men our work in the nursery being nearly completed, the whole of the digging has been done and all is clean and bright.' Bad weather especially frost could stop work altogether:

Monday 27th December 1886 – Truly it has been a bitter night … the immense and unusual fall of snow being in many places drifted to 4 and 5 feet in depth and a general thickness of 12 to 18 inches, all communication with carts is stopped and father had this morning to bring out the horses to trample a road from the farm to the cottages. Martin managed with great difficulty to get up the common to help us make paths it taking him nearly 2 hours to come a usual ½ hour's walk.

The weather continued with frost every night:

Jan 1st 1887 – Such a New Year has not been known for many years as today it is well we should wish each other a happy new year, but the prospects in commencing is certainly gloomy for the poor … Tonight is pay night but we have very little for the poor men they having been unable to do anything but dig out a little gravel and only a few of them have done that.

The variety of plants grown at Heatherside included many trees, roses, ivies, clematis and strawberries as well as the ericaceous plants the nursery became famous for. Strawberries had to be taken to London for sale, and Frederick Street junior describes this experience in detail:

122   *Long Border at Sunningdale*

> 7th July 1885 – I and Father went early this morning to Covent Garden, reached
> there about 4 o'clock to sell the strawberries, what a vast babble and haggling
> … one to sell and another to buy and an immense number ready to step over
> the boundary … to steal and plunder. To sell in Covent Garden market makes
> a man alive to every touch.

On the farm, apart from keeping livestock, the Street's grew hay, potatoes
and mangolds.

On 24 October 1885, Harry, Frederick's younger brother, started working
for Mr Bennett at Shepperton at a salary of 11s. a week. At the end of 1886,
Harry left Bennett's and in February 1887 he was ready for the second stage of
his training. Frederick noted:

> Messrs Jackman of Woking has written very kindly offering him a place …
> being a large nursery he will have every opportunity to learn the whole details
> of the trade, and we have therefore decided to accept their offer and Harry is
> to commence work on March the 7th at the weekly wages of 14/- me making
> Mr Chaplin the propagator a present of £5 after the first year for teaching
> and showing him all he can.

Working for Sir Gabriel Goldney, and later for his sons, caused problems for
the Street family after a small dispute broke out between Sir Gabriel and a neighbour
over access to land. Frederick was caught in the middle and recorded:

> November 1st 1886 – what could poor father do if we had to leave this place
> for a living he has only sufficient money to take a small farm, on which he
> would have to work very hard to obtain a living, and be source of trouble and
> worry to both him and Mother in their old age.

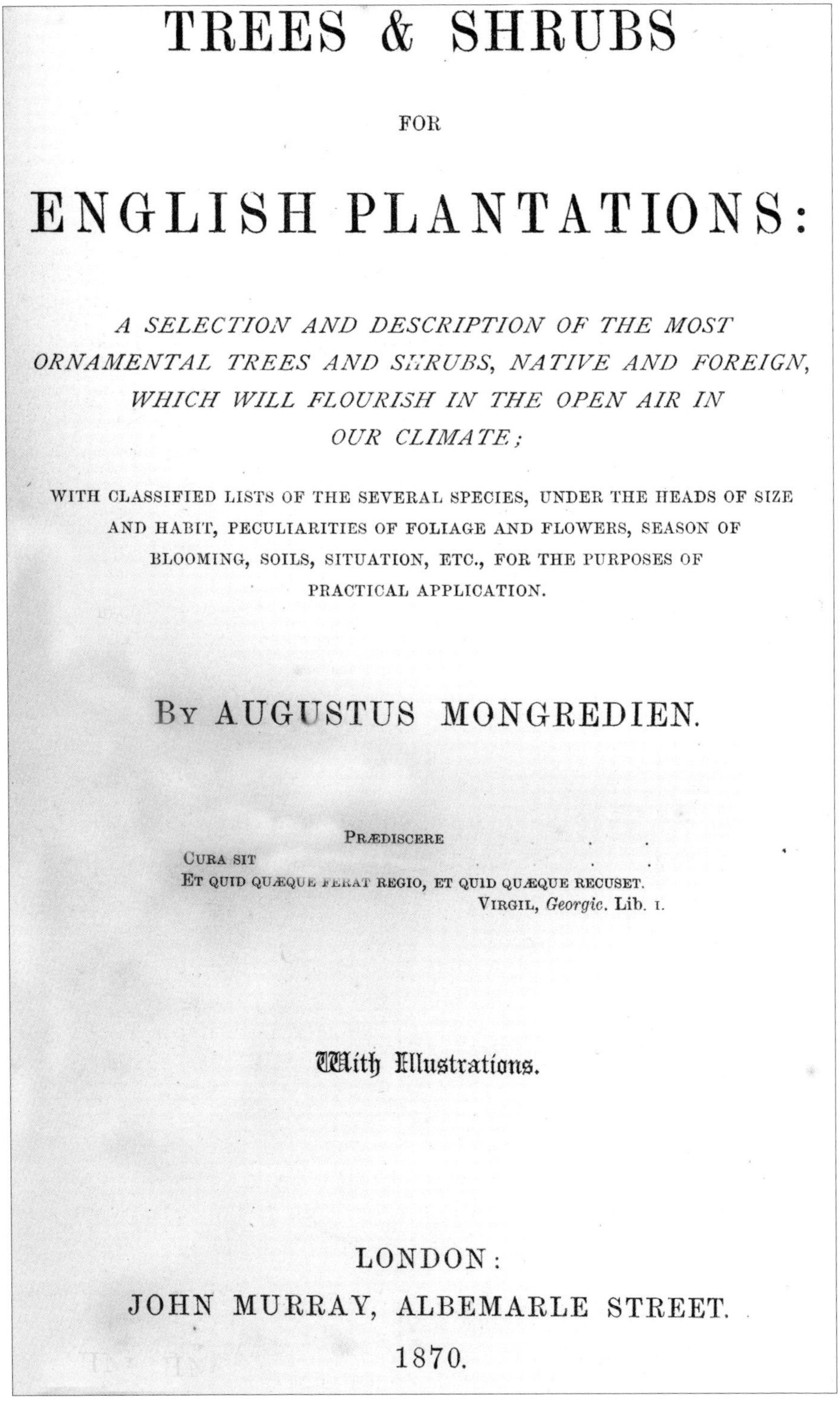

TREES & SHRUBS

FOR

ENGLISH PLANTATIONS:

*A SELECTION AND DESCRIPTION OF THE MOST
ORNAMENTAL TREES AND SHRUBS, NATIVE AND FOREIGN,
WHICH WILL FLOURISH IN THE OPEN AIR IN
OUR CLIMATE;*

WITH CLASSIFIED LISTS OF THE SEVERAL SPECIES, UNDER THE HEADS OF SIZE
AND HABIT, PECULIARITIES OF FOLIAGE AND FLOWERS, SEASON OF
BLOOMING, SOILS, SITUATION, ETC., FOR THE PURPOSES OF
PRACTICAL APPLICATION.

By AUGUSTUS MONGREDIEN.

PRÆDISCERE
CURA SIT
ET QUID QUÆQUE FERAT REGIO, ET QUID QUÆQUE RECUSET.
VIRGIL, *Georgic.* Lib. I.

With Illustrations.

LONDON:
JOHN MURRAY, ALBEMARLE STREET.
1870.

123   *Trees and Shrubs
for English Plantations,
Mongredien, 1870*

The Street family were also required to collect debts for the Goldney's:

> 14th July 1887 – Today we have a sad interview with poor Mrs Stephens at Lightwater … her husband the Doctor contracted a debt with us … today Sir Gabriel sent Father down to insist on having the a/c paid before leaving the house but on his arrival the poor doctor was so ill that he was not expected to last the day over.

The doctor died on 19 July and 'whether any payment will be procured now or not is a question as we hear his family are in great difficulties … he had died also without making a will. It is to be hoped his life is heavily insured.' The doctor owed the Goldney's £70.

By far the most difficult time for Frederick was in March 1889 when Sir Gabriel was an old man and his sons took over the estate. The sons seemed to be under the impression that the Street family were not operating honestly, and Mr Prior Goldney and his brother Frederick accused the Streets of mismanagement of Sir Gabriel's money used by them to improve the land:

> 18th March – such charges have been brought against us today that have never before been laid at our feet … that the whole of the money spent here by their father had been exceedingly ill applied as a paying investment, that all the time and so called skill of ours had been sadly ill used in rearing up an encumbrance on the land and a hindrance to its immediate sale. That the 53 acres of land we have cleared of heath and gorse and tilled and got into a beautiful productive field would now be equally valuable for building land had no money been spent on its and it was still covered with heath and gorse and fir trees and that consequently the money so applied was entirely a dead loss.

Frederick was so upset by the visit of Sir Gabriel Goldney's sons, that he offered to purchase all stock growing on the nursery at cost value, and rent the land on which they grew. The month after he writes his last entry in this wonderful diary:

> My fathers and my own prospects seem now for the moment entirely floundered we had cherished the idea and prospect of building a substantial trade here that would repay all parties fairly … but now we are told or rather hinted at that the whole of the land and premises would be sold tomorrow if a customer came … and that then our services would be no longer required … With these prospects in front of one is it not time we made or provided some surer home or refuge that we might fly to whenever this may happen?

Many landowners in Camberley were attempting to sell off plots of land for housing, including Charles Raleigh Knight and the Pain family at Deepcut. Very few deals went ahead, and as little of the Heatherside estate was sold the Streets did not have to move and Frederick took over the management of it from the death of his father in 1906. During the First World War, Frederick, unlike most nurserymen who retained staff by growing vegetables, put forward his case to the Tribunal:

It is in the national interest that Ellis should be allowed to remain at his present occupation. The man is absolutely necessary to the business, which is engaged in capturing trade that has hitherto been carried on by Germany with America … my firm is getting ready from £6,000 to £7,000 worth of rhododendrons for exportation to America in February and March whilst another firm of nurserymen had obtained an order for 765,000 rose bushes for America.[22]

In 1926, the Goldney family offered Frederick Street a short-term lease which did not suit him. Heatherside was taken on by William King who had started work there as a boy in March 1887, and Frederick moved to West End. In 1906, the farm had been sold to the Stokes family who, until the early 21st century, operated Heatherside Dairy in Park Street, a reminder of the early days when their cows had grazed in fields where so many houses stand today.

CHOBHAM, WEST END AND BISLEY NURSERIES

When he left Heatherside, Frederick Street purchased a small nursery in Fenns Lane, West End, which had been owned by Denis Heather. Fenns Lane Nursery specialised in growing kalmias, rhododendrons and azaleas on just 10 acres of the 30-acre holding. Frederick changed the name to Heathermead and grew ericaceous plants, which he wrote about in the books he had published on their propagation, and he also wrote the history of the Goldsworth Nursery. After the death of Frederick Street in 1942, Heathermead nursery was left to his sister Alice, under the management of Harry Free.[23] Frederick's nephew Frederick John Street, usually known as John, was the son of Herbert Street. John started work in 1932 at Allgrove's in Langley and later moved to Waterer's at Bagshot where he became an assistant manager. In 1942, John Street leased the 11-acre site from his Aunt Alice and gradually restored the nursery after the war, he also established a traditional 'English' landscape garden around the house – a smaller version of the one set out at Heatherside by Augustus Mongredien. John was an expert plantsman who became as famous for his books, magazine articles and television and radio interviews as he did for his plants. He exhibited at all the major shows and it was his rhododendrons that lined part of the route through London at the Coronation of Queen Elizabeth II in 1954. The Heathermead nursery closed in 1985.

John's uncle, Henry Street, founded the Surrey Rose Nursery at Bullhousen in Bisley, where he also farmed, and by 1922 he had moved to Fordville in the same village. Henry Street's training at Bennett's in Shepperton and at Jackman's in Woking, as well as his experience as a child growing up at Heatherside, stood him in good stead as a businessman, and in 1924 he moved to West End, initially at Pennypot. Later, Henry Street purchased land to the west of Guildford Road in West End, where the nursery flourished until it was sold for development in 1986. Although best known for its roses, Street's West End nursery also grew ericaceous shrubs, ornamental and flowering trees and hedge plants.

After Henry Street's death, his wife Amy took over the running of the business with the assistance of her daughter Mollie, who had married Reginald Goold, the son of the head gardener at Hillcrest estate in Camberley. Mollie and Reginald Goold's son, Harry, took over the nursery in turn. He was passionately interested in and knowledgeable about the plants grown, especially the roses for which the nursery was renowned. When interviewed in 1998, Harry was willing to explain the principles by which the nursery trade had been managed since foundation, having no doubt heard, or been party to, conversations from members of his family and other nurserymen from a small boy:

> Nearly all the work was piece-work, and the great labourers in the nursery were the people who dug clay in the summer for the brickworks and in the winter they'd come and dig the ground for the nurserymen ... everyone in West End was multi-skilled ... now the really clever guys would ... go round cutting hay and all these other jobs as the season progressed ... piecework planting – that's why West Enders were so well known; they were very hard workers, very skilled manual workers.

Harry Goold also gave a view on how many of the smaller nurseries started in business and how some workmen supplemented their income: 'All the nurseries, they grew up by dinner-bagging ... well, they came with their dinner in a bag and went home with the governor's cuttings and then sold them back to the governor.'[24] Surrey Rose Nursery moved from the village to Arborfield in 1986 when the land was sold for development, where it is still a family business run by the fourth generation of this remarkable family.

124 *Frederick Street jnr, writer of the Heatherside diary*

Numerous smaller, specialised or independent nurserymen operated in Surrey Heath; some were local boys like Carmi Cobbett and his brother Henry, who set up a nursery just over the border of the parish in Horsell, and others were like John Anthony Straver, who came from Holland to work for Henry Street at Surrey Rose Nursery in 1927. John Straver met a Mr Van der Vis of Booksop who had an exporting firm, became his representative in England, and they set up the Roseland Nursery in Bagshot Road, West End in the 1930s. In the 1950s, John Straver became the sole owner of the company and after his death in 1979, John's eldest son took over the business. The range of plants sold were expanded, and additional land was purchased until almost 200 acres was cultivated.[25] Another nurseryman who arrived in West End from Booksop was Isaac Bos, who set up his Hagthorne Cottage Nursery in 1966 in Lucas Green Road. Today, Hagthorne Cottage Nursery offers a selection of plants including ferns, bamboos and acers grown by Isaac's son Richard, who took over from his father after his death in 1987.

George Underwood had originally been a propagator for Frederick Street at Heathermead nursery in West End. Underwood married Connie Berry, who grew up at Heatherside where her father George had been the foreman at the nursery. The Hookstone Green nursery of G. Underwood and Son specialised in hardy heaths and brooms, raising many new varieties, and during the 1960s put on fine displays at the Chelsea Flower Show. George Underwood died in 1960 and his wife Connie and son Ken continued to run the business. In the 1960s, George Underwood's brother Leslie purchased a derelict chicken-farm in the Bagshot Road, West End and opened it as Conifers Nursery.[26]

W. Godfrey and Sons was founded by William Godfrey at Brentmoor Road, West End, in 1921. The original nursery was situated opposite Brentmoor House. William also ran a fruit and vegetable stall at the White Hart Market in Slough. The Godfrey family lived and worked in Brentmoor Road from the time William purchased the property from the Tringham family, until it was sold for re-development in the 1970s. William and Margaret Godfrey had two sons, Reginald and Ronald, and each family member had to work within the business to make it profitable. Margaret would spend hours making wreaths, especially prior to Christmas, a difficult, and often painful task when working with holly. Reginald ran the business from 1950, when his father died, and the business now operates from a site in Hook Mill Lane in Lightwater, run by William,

125   *Rhododendron Field, Heatherside*

126   *Frederick Street, George Berry and staff at Heatherside*

Reginald's son, the third generation of the Godfrey family to trade under the name of W. Godfrey and Son.[27]

Castle Grove Nursery in Scotts Grove Road, Chobham, was established by Richard Higgs in 1923. Known as R.H. Higgs, the nursery grew cut-flowers, which would be taken to Woking Station each evening in a cart destined for Covent Garden, pulled by two bicycles ridden by Bert Rapley and Richard. Preferring traditional farming methods, Higgs employed Bert Hill, of Strawberry Farm in Bisley, to work his fields with a horse-drawn plough. During the Second World War Higgs grew his own tobacco, a practice which almost cost him his life from nicotine-poisoning, as it was not cured correctly. Richard was the first in his family to become a nurseryman, his father being a high-class greengrocer in Kew, and his father-in-law, Bernard Coventry, a collector and recorder of Himalayan plants. Higgs had also worked for the forestry commission in Kashmir and while there collected, took photographs of and wrote papers on local plants. Peter and Robin, Richard's sons, took over the family business in the 1950s when it was still best known for salad crops and cut-flowers. Peter and Robin introduced bedding-plants and a fine range of roses, employing many Italians from the area around Naples who worked at budding roses for them which were then sold, bare root, in bundles of twenty-five. Peter introduced the concept of patio plants and Robin concentrated on his much-loved roses.[28]

One of the largest employers of local men was Thomas Hilling, who set up in business in Chobham at the same time as Richard Higgs but with an entirely different ethos – he employed all the latest machinery available. In 1952, Hilling stood as a local councillor and won the seat by a huge majority of almost 1,000 votes. He was also the first local man to employ Graham Stuart Thomas. One of the smaller nurseries was Percy Small's; Percy and his brother Ron were well-known in West End and Percy became very involved in the local community as a Parish Councillor and Trustee of the Poor. He was also well-versed in how nurserymen used the produce of the heath. The Small family inherited the nursery at King's Road from their father and, although the nursery closed when they retired, their nephew Robert is still a nurseryman at North Hill Nurseries in Scotts Grove Road.[29]

Almost all of the men who set up their own business had worked for other nurserymen or in large gardens. Robert Glazier, who founded Elm Tree Nursery in West End in 1923, did so after working with patients in the gardens of Brompton Sanatorium at Frimley during the First World War. Glazier had set up in business just after the war as a smallholder with a few cows at Linton in Lucas Green, growing nursery plants on part of his land, and he bought the site of Elm Tree Nursery in Guildford Road in 1923 from Herbert Gosden. Elm Tree Nursery, later run by Robert Glazier's eldest son William, continued to trade until the 1990s. Robert's younger son, Arthur, started work at Slocock's in 1926, and in 1936, when he went to work for Collyer's nursery in Carthouse Lane, Bisley, he was earning 38s. a week. Arthur Glazier's hours were from 7am to 5pm in winter, 7am to 5.30pm in summer and to 1pm on Saturdays. If he did 'piece' work he could earn up to £3 a week, for budding roses he received 1s. 10d. a hundred – over 3,000 would have to be worked a week to earn £3. Arthur recalled that men never sat down without having a budding knife in their hands. After the Second World War Arthur Glazier founded Newbridge nursery in Bisley, where he specialised in growing roses for the wholesale trade. There was a local

127   *Mr Gunner at the Surrey Rose Nursery stand*

128 *Reginald Godfrey, Alan Haywood and friend, Godfrey's nursery, Brentmoor Road, 1950s*

syndicate that purchased 6,000,000 stocks of roses from Holland each year, which were grown on by local nurserymen.[30]

Another man to have worked for the Collyer's and at Hilling's was Jack Elliott, who set up on his own in Fenns Lane in 1936. Initially, Jack and his wife grew vegetables with a little nursery stock, which enabled them to continue in business throughout the Second World War. Known as J.W. Elliott and Sons, the business changed its name in 1946 to Fenns Lane Nursery, where the Elliott family concentrated on increasing the range of plants grown. Two of their sons, John and Ron, followed their parents into the business.[31]

At Bisley, two nurseries were set up specialising in conifers. At Queens Road in Bisley, Geoffrey Bramley-Ball, who started his working life with Thomas Hilling, purchased five acres of land at Wisdom Nursery. From the age of 39, Bramley-Ball was handicapped by losing his sight, but was still able to take cuttings and prepare plants, aided by a nursery foreman who lived on site. Around the corner at Bisley Green, John and Marjorie Tilbury established their three-acre Lincluden nursery in the late 1980s, and with little additional labour were able to show their unusual forms of conifer plants at all major shows, winning 48 gold medals by 2003.

129 *Higgs Nursery*

130 *George Berry, foreman at Heatherside*

131 *Hillings staff, 1950s: Ted Slaughter, Horry Collyer, Kath Underwood and Jimmy Coombes*

Surrey Heath became home to great plantsmen including Sir Joseph Hooker and Graham Stuart Thomas. When Sir Joseph retired as Director of Kew he moved to Windlesham, where he planted a magnificent garden surrounding his home, The Camp, in Westwood Road. Graham Stuart Thomas lived at West End, where he also planted a garden around his home in Fairfield Lane.

Today, a number of nurseries and garden centres still employ large numbers of local men and women. Longacres, a business established by Peter Long in the late 1970s in Bagshot, is a modern garden centre, offering a wide variety of plants and related products. Other nurseries, including Jackson's and Plants Limited in Chobham, offer a wholesale service to landscape-gardeners and larger markets. Wholesale nurseries exist beside the traditional long-standing businesses that have been in Surrey Heath for generations, which between them have a pool of expertise second to none.

132 *John Rose with winning 'Johnny Rose' rhododendron*

Chapter Eight

LARGE HOUSES AND ESTATES

In Surrey Heath, many opportunities existed to work as a servant. Most were employed at the royal households or the homes of gentry, especially those attracted in the earlier period. Later on, further opportunities arose for servants in the military and other institutions.

In the 19th and 20th centuries, working as a servant was predominately an occupation where women outnumbered men, and in Surrey Heath it was almost the only occupation in which women could be sure of finding work. In the parish registers for Windlesham, between 1840 and 1849 there are 115 marriages, with 82 of the women giving their occupation as servants; of the remaining women, six were widows, two were dressmakers and one a milliner. There are no occupations given for the remainder of the women, so at least 70 per cent relied on earning their income as servants. In the 1851 Census for Surrey Heath villages, at least 350 people are enumerated as servants, charwomen, housekeepers and laundresses.

It was always considered a sign of wealth that households could employ male rather than female servants, and it is these men who first appear in the parish registers. No male servants are recorded in the extant registers for Chobham as they post-date the time when the Royal residence, Chobham Park, was at its zenith. At Bagshot in 1791, Henry Bartholomew was house-steward to Ralph Leycester at Hall Grove, and Joseph Child was gamekeeper to the Prince of Wales at Bagshot Park.[1] Wealthier employers, or the upwardly mobile, employed staff from outside the immediate area, perhaps in an attempt to stop 'house gossip' from circulating around the village. At Bagshot Park in 1851, 13 staff were living-in, none were local. At nearby Hall Grove, only one of six servants, Jane Goodman, a young kitchen maid, was local, as she was born in Guildford. At Chobham Place, all 10 servants were from other areas, as were the three at Westcroft Park. Of five people employed at Woodlands House in Windlesham, only William Howard from Bisley was born locally.

Servants moved around the country, because the household moved, or due to poor working conditions or lack of commitment to the household. For servants who settled down to long-term work with a family, the village became 'theirs'; either they met a partner and married, or they had the benefits of living-in, with good food and adequate shelter for their working life and perhaps an annuity at

133 *Bagshot Park*

the end of it. Bagshot Park was an estate where servants tended to stay on, and two widows, Mary Bowdery, aged 83, and Rebecca Wickens, aged 55, were both drawing pensions from the estate in 1851. Both the Bowdery and Wickens families continue to live in Surrey Heath today.

In 1928 there were still 17 gardeners, two keepers, all the farm staff, chauffeurs, grooms, indoor servants, indoor and outdoor carpenters and a night watchman employed at Bagshot Park.[2] The only known diary of a person 'in service' in local households is *From Hall-Boy to House-Steward*, the life of William Lanceley, published by Edward Arnold and Co. in 1925. Lanceley was born in 1854 and went in to service at the age of 16 as a hall-boy to the local squire, he eventually served as house-steward to Lord Roberts at the Curragh, before arriving to take up a similar position within the household of the Duke of Connaught at Bagshot Park. Lanceley's diary describes the hierarchy within the servants' quarters, and the food and ale in abundance for all, as he worked his way up through the households to reach the pinnacle of the profession, serving the son of the Queen.

SERVANTS TO TRADESMEN

The poorest servants were those who worked for up-and-coming tradesmen, or those attached to beerhouses, and this could be a much more precarious living compared to the lives of servants in large houses or estates. In the Quarter Sessions records and the parish vestry meetings, the movements of many of less fortunate servants were scrutinised, usually as they fell into need, requiring vestry handouts. The examinations to prove a last place of settlement highlight how people were employed, and their life at work. One local example is Charlotte Taplin, who in January 1836 described herself as a single woman living in Egham. The Egham parish authorities wished to return Taplin to Chobham. She said:

On the 13th February 1832 I went into the service of Mr Richardson publican at Chobham as his indoor servant I was hired by the year at £5 a year I served under such hiring in Chobham for 15 Months and then left his service … I lived in no Service since for 12 Months or done any act to acquire a settlement … I have received relief from the parish of Egham and am become chargeable.[3]

In Yorktown Charlotte Taplin would probably have found work. Tradesmen supplying services to the college were able to provide their wives with a general servant who was usually young and inexperienced, although their wives were probably not far removed from this way of life themselves. In 1851 at Yorktown, 15-year-old Elizabeth Parker of Frimley and 19-year-old Ann Grinham of Crookham were both working for Frederick Look the baker, and his wife; and Clara Carrington, aged 13, was a general servant in the household of John Farrell, the tailor. Local girls were employed because confidentiality was not such a consideration in smaller households, as in large establishments, and they would have been far cheaper to employ. An alternative to employing local girls was to employ a widow who needed to find accommodation and was used to household work; invariably they were termed housekeepers rather than servants.

ORPHANAGES AND INSTITUTIONS

The availability of cheap land meant that by the end of the 19th century, new large establishments were built that required many domestic staff in the vicinity of all the villages. The Shaftesbury Farm School opened at Bisley in 1868, followed in 1873 by the Shaftesbury School. The schools were branches of the national charity with its headquarters in London, which took advantage of the space available in this

134   *Connaught Lodge and entrance to Bagshot Park.*

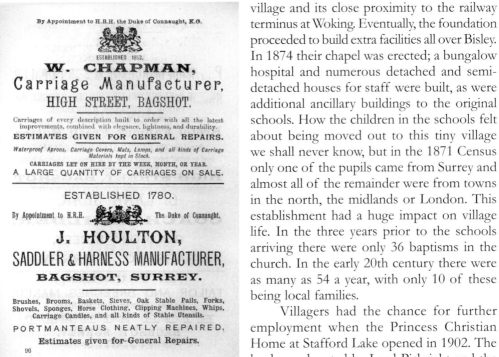

135 *Tradesmen in Bagshot relied on Royal patronage*

village and its close proximity to the railway terminus at Woking. Eventually, the foundation proceeded to build extra facilities all over Bisley. In 1874 their chapel was erected; a bungalow hospital and numerous detached and semi-detached houses for staff were built, as were additional ancillary buildings to the original schools. How the children in the schools felt about being moved out to this tiny village we shall never know, but in the 1871 Census only one of the pupils came from Surrey and almost all of the remainder were from towns in the north, the midlands or London. This establishment had a huge impact on village life. In the three years prior to the schools arriving there were only 36 baptisms in the church. In the early 20th century there were as many as 54 a year, with only 10 of these being local families.

Villagers had the chance for further employment when the Princess Christian Home at Stafford Lake opened in 1902. The land was donated by Lord Pirbright and the home was built as a workshop for disabled servicemen. Although establishments brought trained staff of their own, additional local people were needed to undertake unskilled work. Staff with the ability to cook or garden, tidy and clean rooms, make general repairs, or to keep down the huge pile of laundry were required. The homes also employed local office staff.

In addition to the employment opportunity that the Princess Christian Home and Shaftesbury Schools provided, many Bisley men were able to get work at the new Brookwood Asylum, including William Searle in 1884 and Harry Hill in the 1890s. Not that this was always considered a good move as Frederick Street of Heatherside Nursery noted in his diary after a visit from Harry Hill:

> Thursday 18th June 1885 – He is one of the attendants at Brookwood asylum.
> I fear there is but little chance of his rising much above his present position
> as in a place of that kind one is neither learning useful knowledge nor making
> himself skilled in anything but cutting up food and making beds![4]

The Gordon Boys' School at West End was built as a national memorial to General Gordon, initially for boys who had lost at least one parent and especially for boys whose fathers had served in the army; they were not young children, some arrived from other orphanages or had been recommended to the school by people worried for their welfare, and some had been working at menial jobs to help the family budget.

At The Gordon Boys' School students were trained in trades suitable for their eventual entry into the army; they were taught tailoring, baking and bootmaking, and those with aptitude were taught to play musical instruments. Not all boys made it in to the army, but most did, and those that chose not to enter it at least had additional skills where they could find better employment after leaving than if they had not attended the school.

Local men were employed to teach the boys gardening and how to grow vegetables, how to breed and look after pigs, and even how to make a good job of cleaning windows. The produce from the farm and fields were used to feed the hungry boys. As with all of large institutions, the school was erected on a corner of heathland unsuited for growing a profitable farm crop. While The Gordon Boys' School did not expand to take over the village, as the Shaftesbury School did in Bisley, it does have a chapel, housing for staff and a library built within its grounds.

An example of the intake of boys to the school can be gauged from boy no. 26, William Henry Dettmar, whose father was a looking-glass frame maker of Hackney, whose mother had died. William was aged 15 and just 4ft 10in in height when he arrived in October 1885 and had already been employed in Mr Horrocks' Glass Blowing Works earning a wage of 6s. a week. William was recommended to the school by the Eton Mission of Hackney, and spent two years at the school before joining the Royal Artillery.[5] It must have been extremely strange for a boy brought up in a poor working-class home, used to the bustle and dirt of city life, to arrive in such an ordered and quiet environment, and the role of the house-parents must have been a difficult one.

The Royal Albert Orphanage, between Bagshot and Frimley, was built as a memorial to Prince Albert who had died on the 14 December 1861 after being taken ill planting a tree at the Staff College on 22 November. Although the Prince did not die immediately, he was weakened by the chill. It is said that Queen Victoria subsequently paid only one visit to the town, when she laid the foundation stone to the Chapel and planted a Wellingtonia tree in the grounds of this orphanage on 29 June 1867.

136 *Farm school and chapel, Bisley*

137 *Tailor's workshop, Shaftesbury School, 1940s*

The Royal Albert Orphanage was initially for boys and girls, and of the first intake of 102 children in 1864, 50 were boys and 52 girls. The orphanage was housed in a partially completed property known as Collingwood Court, an alternative name used when it was referred to locally. A farm was established in the extensive grounds of the orphanage which reached from the Portsmouth Road to the Upper Chobham Road, where the children were taught to work the land and to look after animals. The children were also taught useful trades, which for girls included household skills, and for boys were those similar to other establishments, such as bootmaking and tailoring. Housing for orphanage staff was built at the southern entrance to the grounds near the junction of Upper Chobham Road and the Maultway. The Royal Albert Orphanage was known as The Royal Albert School by the 1940s.[6]

HEALTH BENEFITS

It had been known for many years that in areas with plantations of pine trees, the air would be good for those suffering from chest diseases. In 1898, Sadler & Baker, the Camberley estate agents, produced a brochure which was sent to military men serving abroad, encouraging them to retire to the town. Entitled the *Archachon of England* the brochure used quotes from various publications to highlight the advantages:

> The climate of Camberley is considered to be similar to that of Arcachon, which is in the centre of the pine district of the South of France, to which so many journey from England suffering from asthma, chronic catarrh, and chest complaints – all such have been relieved or cured. In the great pine district of the Gironde, those engaged in the work of collecting resin enjoy entire immunity from consumption, which is attributed to the resinous air.

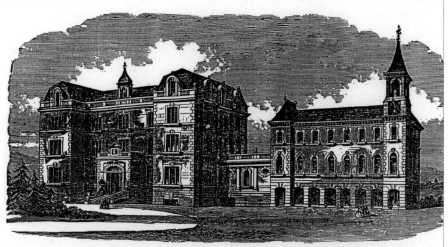

The Royal Albert Orphan Asylum,

FOR THOROUGHLY DESTITUTE CHILDREN,

COLLINGWOOD COURT, NEAR BAGSHOT, SURREY.

OFFICE—98, CHEAPSIDE, LONDON, E.C.

Patron—HER MAJESTY THE QUEEN.

The Committee do not intend to raise these children above that sphere which the providence of God has marked them out to fill, but in giving them a simple education, consisting of reading, writing, and rudimentary arithmetic, and in teaching them the truths of the Bible, trust they may go forth as honest and industrious children, capable of earning their own livelihood and of proving themselves useful members of society.

To this end *THE GIRLS* are trained to become industrious and useful servants. In addition to the usual household work, they are taught washing and ironing, and especial attention is paid to their being made *efficient in plain and useful needlework.*

THE BOYS are taught to make themselves useful in the house, the kitchen-garden, and upon the farm, where they are gradually reclaiming a portion of the uncultivated land, but in order to meet the necessity which exists for the boys having a more extended sphere of employment, the Committee have erected Workshops for teaching them an elementary knowledge of Bootmaking and Tailoring.

The children are elected by the Subscribers. About two weeks before each Election a List of Candidates, with a short narrative of each case, is forwarded to the Subscribers for them to select the children to be admitted, and thus the most necessitous and deserving objects are certain of securing the benefits of the Asylum.

To ensure this a new and important element is introduced into the constitution of this Institution, viz. *NO CANVASSING FOR VOTES IS ALLOWED;* it being apparent that the destitute have neither friends to devote the time nor the money to spend, which the canvassing system necessitates, and, to prevent the possibility of canvassing, the Reports are published without the addresses of the Subscribers.

The Elections take place half-yearly, in May and November.

Children are received from all parts of the Kingdom, and are admitted between the age of 6 and 12, the boys remaining until 14 and the girls until 15.

Subscriptions for the maintenance of the Orphans are earnestly solicited and will be thankfully received by the Secretary, at the Office, 98, CHEAPSIDE, LONDON, E.C.

sentation—A Donation of £250 in one sum, or subscribed in various sums during a period three years, entitles the Donor to have one child always in the Asylum, provided, of course, within the prescribed conditions.

138 *Royal Albert Orphanage*

139   *The Arcachon of England, 1898*

It also quoted from *The Lancet* of June 1873:

> How few are aware that the locality is one of the very healthiest in England
> and greatly superior as a resort for the invalid … All the surrounding region
> has long been known to the profession as unexceptional in soil and natural
> drainage: while the air has special advantages which recommend it to all, but
> especially to those whose pulmonary organs are weak. The late Sir James Clark
> occupied the Royal Residence in Bagshot Park to the day of his death and was
> never tired of praising its salubrious advantages.

The health benefits of the area no doubt encouraged not only extra employment
for builders who erected the large detached houses for unhealthy people, but also
provided further work for those 'in service'.

It may have been articles similar to that quoted in *The Lancet* which influenced
those looking for out-hospitals for patients to decide to purchase land in Frimley.
The Brompton Sanatorium and the Burrow Hill Colony were both built on
former heathland surrounded by pines for people suffering from chest diseases.
Prior to the introduction of drugs to cure tuberculosis, the only treatment
available to patients was to live and work in fresh air in areas where pine trees
grew. The Brompton Sanitorium and the Burrow Hill Colony had to be open to
the elements as much as possible and kept very clean; therefore large numbers
of local residents found employment there. Some men, who had worked in
either the nursery industry or as agricultural labourers, were taken on to work
with the patients in the gardens of the sanatoria. Brompton Sanatorium, which

In the "MORNING POST" of March, 1883, there appeared a letter from a physician on the Camberley district, in which he says:

"As a physician I am asked day after day where is the best quarter to go for quickly recruiting the health, or where is the healthiest spot to reside in and within a handy distance of town. What I can and do tell them may be a boon to many others to know. *Nowhere within 100 miles of London is there such dry and bracing air, and it is marvellous to witness how rapidly tubercular affections of the chest, asthma, deranged livers, and rheumatic gout in all its forms there disappear.* I formerly sent many to Scotland or abroad, but happily there is a better than either at hand. To the north of the Chobham Ridges, and westward of the Duke of Connaught's, are several square miles of the wildest and most charming scenery of forest and heath land, belonging to various parishes, kept open for ever under Her Majesty's Inclosure Commissioners. *Heath land is healthier than grass or cultivated land, in so far that heather absorbs but little moisture, and there is barely any decay in it.*"

A medical gentleman well acquainted with Camberley, in an interview with our Editor, said:

"For delicate children with a strumous tendency one cannot conceive any place more suitable; in fact, chest affections, particularly those in an incipient stage, would be greatly benefited by a residence in this locality.

140 *Testimonial to health, 1898*

141 *Brompton Sanatorium*

142   *Patients working in grounds of Brompton Sanatorium*

was attached to the London Hospital of the same name, was erected on land purchased from the Goldney family, which had formed part of their Heatherside Estate, for the sum of £3,900 in 1900.[7]

Burrow Hill Colony was built to house the growing number of men returning from the trenches in The First World War with tuberculosis. In May 1920, the *Camberley News* reported that a 'Farm Colony for the disabled … training soldiers and sailors suffering from tuberculosis … is being established for the training of men in open-air work, such as farming, fruit growing, vegetable growing and outdoor work'. Erected to accommodate 40 men, the 113 acres of the Burrow Hill Colony were considered 'one of the healthiest and most beautiful spots'. The men who stayed at the sanatorium built many of the wooden buildings they lived in, and a farm bailiff was employed to instruct them in farming techniques.

The Baldwin Brown Nursing Home was situated at the top of Prior Hill at Heatherside. Formerly known as Prior Place, the nursing home was a mansion owned and occupied by the Goldney family. In September 1924, Dr Harry Blandford purchased the estate and extended the building as a recuperative home for patients. In 1948, the home was purchased by Kings College Hospital, London, which moved here from Herne Bay in Kent.[8]

Smaller than the Baldwin Brown Nursing Home, but no less important, a home was provided for children at Clearsprings in Macdonald Road, Lightwater, which opened in July 1931 as an out-hospital for their main facility at Paddington Green.[9] Macdonald Road was an area already known for nursing invalids, as Mrs Channes of Wilmhurst advertised in the *Camberley News* as 'an ex VAD nurse who offers a home to a Chronic Invalid, lady or gentleman … Bungalow amongst the pines in two acres of land – 2½ gns Night fees extra.'[10]

In addition to those suffering from disease, children who required a holiday from soot-blackened London were also given respite in the clean fresh air of the Surrey Heath area. In 1916, a Summer Holiday Crèche was established at Conewood, Camberley, which was lent to the National Society of Day Nurseries by William Watson so that children could 'spend their days in the open air amongst the pines'.[11] As with other large establishments opened locally, professional staff arrived from other parts of the country to work at the Crèche and Nursery, although the work in clearing the land, building the premises and the eventual service tasks would have provided employment for local people. Visitors to these institutions added to the numbers of people buying goods in village shops, visiting pubs and using service trades such as taxis. Cottagers or market gardeners arranged for eggs, flowers and fresh fruit to be available as visitors got off the train or walked to visit relatives. Visitors generally did not know the area, and for the majority, sadly, it was usual that the purpose of the visit was to see a sick relative or an orphaned child.

ARTISTS

There is a long history of people attracted to the Surrey Heath area for its beauty. Living out on the heathland in the late 17th century was a man referred to by the writer John Aubrey:

> At the end of this Hundred I must not forget my noble Friend Mr Charles Howard's Cottage of Retirement (which he called his Castle) which lay in the Middle of a vast Heathy Country, far from any Road or Village in the Hope of a Heathy Mountain, where in troublesome Times, he withdrew from the Wicked World, and enjoyed himself here, where he had only one Floor, his little Dining Room, a Kitchen, a Chapel, and a Laboratory. His Utensils were all of Wood or Earth; near him were about half a Dozen Cottages more.[1]

143 *Interior of Brompton Sanatorium*

149

144   *Burrow Hill Colony, for men from the First World War with tuberculosis*

Aubrey paints a rather romantic view of a man who could undoubtedly have lived a more luxurious life if he had wished, but for some this was the only way to have any kind of home.

In the 19th century, Deepcut, Frimley and Frimley Green attracted a small colony of artists and writers, some of whom are commemorated in Frimley Church. John Frederick Lewis R.A., known as 'Spanish' Lewis, came to Frimley as a child in the early 19th century as his aunt married the Rector of Frimley, Charles Stonehouse. It is not known how much time Frederick and his siblings spent in Frimley, but he was buried there in August 1876 and one of the stained glass windows in the church is in his memory.[13]

Dame Ethel Smyth, the suffragette and composer, arrived at Frimhurst in Frimley Green in 1867, whilst her father, Major-General J.H. Smyth, was in command of the Artillery at Aldershot. Dame Ethel Smyth recalled her childhood memories of living in the village in *Impressions that Remained*; she played the organ and was a member of the choir at St Peter's in Frimley, as an adult she moved to Frimley and lived at One Oak in Portsmouth Road. There is a memorial plaque in her memory in the church.[14]

Charles Wellington Furse moved to Heatherside for a different reason as he was suffering from tuberculosis, and the pine trees and elevated position of the site on which he built his home were considered beneficial. Furse purchased the land for Yockley House from the Goldney's in 1899, married in 1900, and only

145   *Heathland view in Camberley, 1899, from a Sadler & Baker brochure*

lived in the house for four years when he died as his wife gave birth to their second son. Furse's painting 'Diana of the Uplands', on display in the Tate Gallery, is of his wife on the heathland near to where they lived. He was buried at St Peter's Church in October 1904.[15]

Hamo Thorneycroft, the sculptor, was another artist attracted to Deepcut, who moved with his wife and family into Highbridge, beside the Basingstoke Canal in May 1891. Thorneycroft's children were able to enjoy the freedom of living in open countryside and they were called back for meals by a maid who blew on a large cow-horn to recall them; the family lived in Deepcut until 1899.[16]

The Pain family owned most of the land in Deepcut and much of the former heathland at Frimley Green. Robert Tucker Pain, third son of Edward Pain, lived in Deepcut. Robert had Overdale and Fairseat built and took a remarkable set of early photographs of the area, which he used for inspiration in his paintings; the photographs are now held at Surrey Heath Museum and examples have been used to illustrate this book.

CONCLUSION

Today Surrey Heath is a thriving area; the eastern side of the borough is made up of the villages of Bisley, Chobham and Windlesham, while to the west, Camberley is a fairly large town with industrial estates along the Blackwater Valley.

During the 1940s, a decision was made by the Frimley and Camberley Urban District Council to redevelop the town of Camberley and take in some of the 'overspill' from the Metropolitan boroughs of Surrey: Sutton, Cheam, Wimbledon, Surbiton, Kingston and Esher. Camberley did not become a 'new town', as much of the land surrounding it was owned by the War Office and they did not wish to sell it. Initially, new estates were built for local people at Old Dean and James Road and people were moved out from the town centre to these new estates. Schools and churches were built for the new estates and those in the town centre were demolished to make way for shops. Rorkes Drift Estate at Mytchett and Ansell Estate at Frimley were built for the 'overspill', and extensions to James Road and Old Dean provided more accommodation for them. New factories were also built, and 'key-worker' housing was erected. With the opening of the M3 in the early 1970s the area became a commuter town.

Frimley's old village, lined with Georgian houses and traditional shops, was demolished to provide wider streets and a supermarket. A new hospital was erected in place of the cottage hospital, now too small to cope. Lightwater, and the land between the village and Bagshot, became a prime place to build new housing. The largest of the institutions were closed and the land was built on.

At Chobham, with no railway station and no major through-traffic, the village has expanded over time but without the pressure put on other villages, partly because the majority of the land was either good for agriculture or overseen by the Chobham Common Preservation Society. With little industry to bring wealth and a fairly constant local population, houses in Chobham were rarely demolished; a few were modernised, but these were the exception. Today, Chobham is still a village and has the greatest number of listed buildings in Surrey Heath.

The ancient villages of West End and Bisley have suffered blight from the busy roads, which cut through the heart of each with settlements either side. By contrast Lightwater, the newest of the villages, retains a village feel with its by-pass. Change brings heartache for some and opportunity for others.

Most heathland has now been built over, estates have encroached, and our pet cats and dogs disturb the few ground-nesting birds that remain. Currently, a European Directive has been put in place to restrict further building near to what is left of the increasingly rare and precious heathland habitat. At long last we have come to appreciate the wild beauty of this villainous heath!

REFERENCES

ABBREVIATIONS USED IN THE FOOTNOTES

H.R.O.	Hampshire Record Office, Winchester
S.H.C.	Surrey History Centre, Goldsworth Road, Woking
S.H.M.	Surrey Heath Museum, Knoll Road, Camberley
N.A.	National Archives at Kew
N.N.L.	British Library, Colindale
R.L.C.	Museum of English Rural Life, Reading
R. Lib.	Reading Library

All references regarding the 1851 Census are from a database held at Surrey Heath Museum, compiled by the author, of all the Surrey Heath villages.

INTRODUCTION

1. Daniel Defoe, *A Tour Through the Whole Island of Great Britain* (reprint by Penguin, 1971), p.156.
2. S.H.C. G 98/8/6 The Rev. Edward Cooper of Windlesham to Lord Onslow, 16 Oct 1772.

CHAPTER ONE – A FARMING LIFE

1. S.H.C. 361/15/44-144.
2. S.H.C. G 97/5/9/63.
3. S.H.M. Transcript held.
4. H.R.O. Gilbert Neve B21/61, Henry Woods, Hw B 1603 Transcripts held at S.H.M.
5. Copy held at S.H.M.
6. S.H.C. 72/1/1-9 court rolls for Frimley.
7. S.H.M. Henry W. Aldred, *Ancient & Modern History of Frimley* (1896), p.25.
8. H.R.O. 15M50/1034.
9. S.H.C. Miss D.A. Powell (ed.), *Surrey Quarter Sessions 1669-1670*, vol.10.
10. N.A. MH12/12143.
11. R.L.C. R. Bradley, *A complete body of husbandry: collected from the practice and experience of the most considerable farmers in Britain* (1727), p.118.
12. *Ibid.*
13. *Ibid.*
14. S.H.C. 1354/1.
15. E.W. Brayley *et al.*, *A Topographical History of Surrey* (R.B. Ede, 1841-8), p.238.
16. S.H.C. 72/1/1-9 court rolls for Frimley.
17. R.L.C. W.E. Tate, *Enclosure Acts and Awards*.
18. N.A. 30/9/10/24.
19. *Ibid.*
20. R.L.C. William Stevenson, *Agriculture of Surrey* (1809), p.61.
21. N.A. 30/9/10/24.
22. *Ibid.*
23. R.L.C. James Malcolm, *Compendium of Modern Husbandry,* principally written during a survey of Surrey for the Board of Agriculture (1805).
24. R.L.C. A.G. Parton, Surrey Arch. Soc., vol.64 (1967).
25. Brayley, *op. cit.*, p.218.
26. Stevenson, *op. cit.*, p.390.
27. S.H.C. 361/15/44-144.
28. Brayley, *op. cit.*, p.236.
29. S.H.M. Transcript held. *Lascelles v. Lawrence* – Queens Bench, 19 April 1876 L/311.
30. R. Lib. *Berkshire Chronicle*, 5 May 1838.
31. R. Lib. *Reading Mercury* and *Oxford Gazette*, 26 October 1839.
32. S.H.M. Rent Register, Chobham Farms.
33. S.H.M. Lionel Parr's Reminiscences.
34. S.H.M. Rent Register, Chobham Farms.
35. R.L.C. *Royal Commission on the Employment of Children, Young Persons & Women in Agriculture* (1867).
36. S.H.M. Daisy Hills collection.
37. R.L.C. *Royal Commission on Agricultural Labourers Pay* (1907).
38. Allan Jobson, *The Creeping House of Time*, Robert Hale (1977).
39. S.H.M. Copy of letters sent 6 July 1853, held at Museum.
40. N.A. MH12/12270.
41. S.H.M. *Reading Mercury* and *Oxford Gazette*, 3 November 1783.
42. J. Mason, *Cebba's Ham, the Story of Chobham* (1985), p.7.
43. S.H.M. Frederick Street's Diary. Copy held at Museum.
44. S.H.M. Recollections of Mr Cotterall.
45. N.N.L. *County Chronicle*, August 1848.
46. S.H.M. Peter Fuller's Reminiscences of Bisley in the 1930s.
47. S.H.M. Percy Elkins collection.
48. S.H.C. 361/82/4/6 – the cottage has not been identified.
49. N.N.L. *County Chronicle*, 3 April 1849.
50. *Ibid.*

CHAPTER TWO – SUPPLEMENTARY TRADES AND INCOME

1. S.H.C. Calendar of Assize Records, Surrey Indictments (E1 & J1) J. S. Cockburn 1980-2.
2. R.L.C. *Victoria County History*, p.349.
3. H.R.O. George Martyn, B 35/21629.
4. S.H.M. Sale details.
5. S.H.C. 2589/4/4 Inventory of Frimley Workhouse.
6. S.H.M. Tithe map and Award for Frimley, 1842.
7. Heather Toynbee, *Frimley Green – A Village History* (1973).
8. S.H.C. Calendar of Assize Records, Surrey Indictments (E1 & J1) J. S. Cockburn 1980-2.
9. Lucas Charity records V167/99, held at Drapers Company House.
10. Stevenson, *Agriculture of Surrey* (1809), p.374.
11. N.A. E179/258/4 Hearth Tax returns.
12. Burrows family deeds, held privately.
13. R.L.C. *Victoria County History*, p.350.
14. S.H.M. Tithe map and Award for Frimley 1842.
15. S.H.C. Frimley Court Records, 72/1/9
16. P.A.L. Vine, *London's Lost Route to Basingstoke* (1968).
17. H.R.O. 1637B20/1-2.
18. www.heathhist.pbwiki.com, research by Peter Tipton.
19. H.R.O. 15M50/1034.
20. S.H.M. Tithe map and Award for Frimley (1842).
21. S.H.M. *Frimley Parish Magazine* (1896).

CHAPTER THREE – WORKERS ON THE HEATHLAND

1. Information provided by Mr and Mrs B. Cole.
2. *Morning Leader*, 28 October 1910. Copy held by S.H.M.
3. *Ibid.*
4. 1841 Census HO107/1074/1.
5. 1881 Census RG11/0771/81.
6. S.H.M. Stanley Alder, *Work Amongst the Gipsies* (1893).
7. 1891 Census RG12.
8. R. Lib. *Reading Mercury* and *Oxford Gazette*, 4 May 1839.
9. S.H.M. *I Remember Chobham* (1999), p.19.
10. S.H.M. Reminiscences of Peter Fuller.
11. S.H.C G97/5/15/1.
12. S.H.M. Reminiscences of Bathsheba Smith.
13. R. Lib.. *Reading Mercury* and *Oxford Gazette*, 24 December 1859.
14. Original Rate Book on display in Surrey Heath Museum.
15. S.H.C 361/15/3.
16. S.H.C. QS Easter 1770 and Epiph 1819.
17. S.H.M. Original held.
18. *Old West Surrey* (reprint by Phillimore & Co. Ltd, 1999), p.127.
19. *Ibid.*
20. *Ibid.*
21. Joy Mason, *Cebba's Ham, The Story of Chobham* (1985), p.6.
22. S.H.C. P34/12/12.
23. M. Lightbody, *A History of Erl Wood* (Lilly Research, published privately). Copy at S.H.M.
24. S.H.C. 1320/48/3.
25. R. Lib. *Reading Mercury* and *Oxford Gazette*, 17 August 1839.
26. S.H.M. Frederick Street's Diary. Copy held at Museum.
27. S.H.C. 1320/48/7.
28. S.H.M. Ernie Wells' Reminiscences.
29. S.H.M. Chobham Brickworks file.
30. R. Lib. *Reading Mercury* and *Oxford Gazette*, 30 July 1859.
31. S.H.M. Ernie Wells' Reminiscences.
32. S.H.M. Transcript held. *Lascelles v Lawrence* – Queens Bench, 19 April 1876 L/311.
33. S.H.M. Camberley file.
34. S.H.M. *The Stone Cutters – Old Surrey Craft*, Home Review (1945).

35. S.H.M. *Camberley News*, December 1934.
36. N.A. C12/1093/6.
37. S.H.C. 2589/4/12.
38. S.H.C. 2589/3/2 Vestry Minutes.
39. S.H.M. Lionel Parr's Reminiscences.
40. S.H.M. Ernie Wells' Reminiscences.
41. S.H.C. 361/15/140.
42. S.H.M. Lionel Parr's Reminiscences.
43. S.H.M. F.B.P Lory, *Reminiscences of Bagshot 1874-1919*, p.2.
44. S.H.M Ernie Wells' Reminiscences.
45. S.H.C. G97/5/15/16.
46. S.H.M. *Camberley News* (1915).
47. 1881 Census RG11/0770/88.
48. N.A. MH12/12143.
49. S.H.M. Reminiscence file R 269.
50. S.H.M. Schueller Papers.

CHAPTER FOUR – MILITARY USE OF THE HEATHLAND

1. G.M. Hughes, *A History of Windsor Forest, Sunninghill and the Great Park* (1890).
2. S.H.M. D.E. Hall and F. Gretton, *Farnham During the Civil Wars and Interregnum 1642-60*, Jillings papers, p.269.
3. R. Coe, *An Exact Diary … of the progress of Sir William Waller's army – 1644*.
4. G.M. Hughes, *A History of Windsor Forest Sunninghill and the Great Park* (1890), p.269.
5. Stanley A. Williams, *Official Guide to Windsor Castle* (1938), pp.46-7.
6. G.M. Hughes, *A History of Windsor Forest Sunninghill and the Great Park* (1890), pp.269-70.
7. *Ibid.*
8. G.M. Hughes, *A History of Windsor Forest Sunninghill and the Great Park* (1890), p.271.
9. R. Lib.. *Reading Mercury* and *Oxford Gazette*, 3 August 1792.
10. S.H.M. Major G.A. Kempthorne, *An Eighteenth Century Camp of Exercise*.
11. British Library – Map 183q1(7), 1792, W. Faden for the Duke of Richmond.
12. S.H.M. N.A. *Lady's Magazine*, July 1792, Anthony Greenstreet's research.
13. S.H.M. *European Journal*, November 1792, Anthony Greenstreet's research.
14. S.H.M. Copies of opera held at the British Library, A Biographical Dictionary of Actors, Actresses, Musicians, Dancers, Managers and Other Stage Personnel in London, 1660-1800, Anthony Greenstreet's research.
15. N.A. WO78/5822.
16. Oswald Werge, *www.britishempire.co.uk/forces/armyunits/britishcavalry/17thltdragoonswerge*.
17. S.H.M. Document produced at R.M.C.
18. 1801 Census figures for the Manor of Frimley.
19. Hermione Hobhouse, *Prince Albert His Life and Work* (Hamish Hamilton, 1983), pp.47-8.
20. A.R. Goodwin-Austen, *The Staff and the Staff College* (Constable & Company, 1927), p.85.
21. Goodwin-Austen, *op. cit.*, pp.81, 85.
22. N.A. H045/4626.
23. N.A. H045/4626, 9 June 1853. For a full description of this Camp see *Chobham Great Camp 1853*, Surrey Heath History Club.
24. N.A. WO55/1888.
25. N.A. HO45/4626.
26. *Ibid.*
27. N.A.WO33/1.
28. *Ibid.*
29. James Wyld's map of Chobham Camp (1853).
30. 1851 Census.

31. 1841 Census.
32. *Camberley News*, 19 May 1917.
33. 1841 Census.
34. *Norman's Directory of Camberley & District* (1889).
35. *Yorktown St Michael's Parish Magazine* (1899).
36. Family information provided by Mrs Margaret Rawlings.
37. *Camberley News*, 13 May 1916.
38. Family information provided by Mr Vic Deeks.
39. Ivy Potten, *Looking Back in Longing* (1985), pp.48-9.
40. *Victoria County History*, p.363.
41. John Henry Knight, *Reminiscences of a Country Town* (Farnham) (Martin & Sturt, 1909), pp.42-3.
42. S.H.C. G97/5/15/15.
43. S.H.M. Pain collection.
44. John Morley-Clarke, *The History of Blackdown Camp* (1987), p.1.
45. S.H.M. Frimley and Camberley UDC Rate Books.
46. S.H.M. Poulter Diary.
47. S.H.M. Mytchett Place File.
48. 1934 O.S. map.
49. Richard Schegog and Peter Starling, Mytchett Place and Rudolph Hess (Surrey Heath History Club, 2002), pp.21-2.
50. *Camberley News*, 1 May 1915.
51. *Camberley News*, 30 January 1915.
52. *Camberley News*, 27 March 1915.
53. S.H.M. Chancellor & Sons file.
54. *Camberley News*, 19 November 1926.
55. S.H.M. Frimley & Camberley UDC Rate Books.
56. S.H.M. ATS file.

CHAPTER FIVE – THE INFLUENCE OF THE TURNPIKE ROAD

1. George C.B. Poulter, *Golden Farmer* (1934), p.9.
2. *Ibid.*
3. *Ibid.*, p.10.
4. S.H.M. First published 1828, rep. by Egham-by-Runnymede Historical Society (1983).
5. *Pigot and Co.'s National and Commercial Directory 1839*, Facsimile Edition (1993), p.150.
6. John Henry Knight, *Reminiscences of a Country Town* (Farnham) (Martin & Sturt, 1909).
7. William Albert, *The Turnpike Road System in England* (C.U.P., 1972).
8. R. Lib. *Reading Mercury* and *Oxford Gazette*, 17 May 1813.
9. R. Lib. *Reading Mercury* and *Oxford Gazette*, 17 November 1788.
10. R. Lib. *Reading Mercury* and *Oxford Gazette*, 19 October 1839.
11. Frimley Parish registers.
12. George Sturt, *A Farmer's Life*, p.184.
13. H.R.O. 50M63 Box 5.
14. *Ibid.*
15. The Hon. John Byng Torrington, *The Torrington Diaries: Tours through England and Wales, 1781-94*, 4 Vols. (London, Eyre & Spottiswoode, 1934-8).
16. R. Lib. *Reading Mercury* and *Oxford Gazette*, 9 March 1839.
17. S.H.C. Edward Ryde Diaries /1261.
18. *Ibid.*
19. R. Lib. *Reading Mercury* and *Oxford Gazette*, 23 February 1839.
20. R. Lib. *Reading Mercury* and *Oxford Gazette*, 9 March 1839.
21. *Camberley News*, 22 June 1906.
22. Local trade directories.
23. R. Lib. *Reading Mercury* and *Oxford Gazette*, 9 May 1840.
24. R. Lib. *Reading Mercury* and *Oxford Gazette*, 21 July 1849.
25. S.H.C. 2603/1/1.

26. R. Lib. *Reading Mercury* and *Oxford Gazette*, 9 March 1839.
27. R. Lib. *Reading Mercury* and *Oxford Gazette*, 3 February 1849.
28. Frederick Street's Diary, 11 July 1885.
29. John Cannon, *Bagshot Mill* (1983); S.H.M. Bagshot series no. 8, p.1.
30. *Pigot and Co.'s National and Commercial Directory 1839*, Facsimile Edition (1993).
31. R. Lib. *Reading Mercury* and *Oxford Gazette*, 12 August 1854.
32. P.A.L. Vine, *London's Lost Route to Basingstoke* (1968), p.106.
33. S.H.M. Frimley Tithe Map & Award, 1842.
34. R. Lib. *Reading Mercury* and *Oxford Gazette*, 17 March 1849.
35. H.R.O. 1640AD/124 Inventory.
36. S.H.M. Frimley Park file.
37. S.H.M. Extracts from Parish Chest – Schueller Papers.

CHAPTER SIX – TRADITIONAL VILLAGE TRADES

1. S.H.M Mary Bennett, *The Village Post* (2002), p.33.
2. *Pigot and Co.'s National and Commercial Directory 1839*, Facsimile Edition (1993).
3. S.H.C. 72/1/1-9 court rolls for Frimley.
4. R. Lib. *Reading Mercury* and *Oxford Gazette* (1791).
5. G.A. Kempthorne, *Sandhurst, Berks*, C. Slaughter & Son, p.73.
6. Derek Stidder, *Watermills of Surrey* (1990).
7. *Ibid.*
8. *Chertsey Abbey Cartularies*, Surrey Record Soc., vol.12 (1915-33), p.128.
9. Windlesham Parish Registers.
10. *Pigot and Co.'s National and Commercial Directory 1839*, Facsimile Edition (1993).
11. 1851 and 1881 Census.
12. John Cannon, *Bagshot Mill* (1983); S.H.M. Bagshot series no. 8.
13. Derek Stidder, *Watermills of Surrey* (1990).
14. S.H.M. Copy Abstract of Title (1923).
15. S.H.M. Notes in Bagshot Mill file.
16. John Aubrey, *Natural History and Antiquities of the County of Surrey*, vol.3 (Kohler & Coombes, 1975), p.208.
17. S.H.M. undated sale details.
18. Derek Stidder, *Watermills of Surrey* (1990).
19. Brayley, *op. cit.*, p.348.
20. S.H.M. Reminiscences of Fred Benham.
21. Deeds held privately by the Burrows family.
22. J. Hiller, *Old Surrey Water Mills* (1936).
23. *Ibid.*
24. S.H.M. Sale catalogue.
25. Manorial Records Frimley.
26. S.H.M. File Poulter / Windmill.
27. S.H.C. 72/1/1-9 court rolls for Frimley.
28. Aldred, *Ancient and Modern History of Frimley*, p.9.
29. S.H.C. Calendar of Assize Records, Surrey Indictments (E1 & J1) J. S. Cockburn 1980-2.
30. 1881 Census RG11/0771/55.
31. H.R.O. 15M50/1034.
32. S.H.C. Calendar of Assize Records, Surrey Indictments (E1 & J1) J.S. Cockburn 1980-2.
33. S.H.C. Surrey Wills 1595-1608, vol.4.
34. Windlesham Parish registers.
35. S.H.M. Habakkuk Robinson file.
36. S.H.M. Parish Chest extracts – Schueller Papers.
37. Chobham Parish registers.
38. *Pigot and Co.'s National and Commercial Directory 1839*, Facsimile Edition (1993).
39. H.R.O. 15M50/1034.

40. Society of Genealogists – Apprentices 1731-1749.
41. S.H.C. Surrey Wills.
42. S.H.C. 72/1/1-9 court rolls for Frimley.
43. S.H.C. Edward Ryde Diaries /1261.
44. *Pigot and Co.'s National and Commercial Directory 1839*, Facsimile Edition (1993).
45. H.R.O. 15M50/1034.
46. Old Bailey Proceedings, *www.hrionline.ac.uk*, 15 July 1778.
47. *The Observer* report, reprinted in the *Camberley News*, 6 October 1939.
48. Family information provided by Maureen Rawlings.
49. *Norman's Directory of Camberley* (1889).
50. S.H.M. Four Horse Shoes file.
51. S.H.M. West End forge file.
52. Cambridge University Press (1963).
53. S.H.M R169 White Hart file.
54. S.H.M. Parker books.
55. S.H.M. 1879 Rate book.
56. S.H.M. Plan Register.
57. Information provided by Mr Attewell.
58. *Camberley News*, 22 March 1919.
59. W.J. Carman, Channel Island Transport.
60. 1881 Census Rg11/0783/57.
61. *Norman's Directory of Camberley* (1889).
62. *Drew's Directory of Camberley* (1914).
63. Richard Lucock Wilson, *The Pit Sawyers*, Home Words (1945).
64. David and Elizabeth Clark, *Emigrants to New Zealand*, Surrey Heath History Club Newsletter (February 2005), Dennis Seccombe.
65. Tasman District Council New Zealand website.
66. Kelly's and Norman's Directories.
67. S.H.M. Red Cross Society Report. Caldwell papers.
68. *Camberley News*, 2 June 1917.
69. S.H.M. Lionel Parr's reminiscences.
70. S.H.M. Old Dean Common file.
71. S.H.M Chobham Parish records, transcripts held.
72. For a fuller history of the building trade please see Mary Bennett, *Built to Last*, S.H.M.
73. *Camberley News*, 2 August 1919.

CHAPTER SEVEN – NURSERY WORK

1. Universal Directory (1791).
2. S.H.C. 361/15/44-144.
3. *History and Antiquities of the County of Surrey*, vol.3, Manning & Bray (1814).
4. S.H.C. 361/15/116.
5. S.H.M. Waterer's file.
6. Comm. *On the Employment of Children, Young Persons & Women in Agriculture* (1867).
7. S.H.M. Sunningdale Nursery file.
8. *Ibid.*
9. *Ibid.*
10. S.H.M. Fromow nursery file.
11. E.J. Willson, *Nurserymen to the World* (1989).
12. *Ibid.* pp.77-8.
13. S.H.M. Reminiscences of Leo Robinson.
14. L.R. Russell, *Plant Catalogue* (1981).
15. S.H.M. Deeds relating to London Road recreation ground.
16. *Camberley News*, 4 December 1909.
17. Kathleen M. Burgess, *Frimley Park and Tekels Park Estates*, Surrey Heath History Club (2000).
18. Augustus Mongredien, *Trees and Shrubs for English Plantations* (John Murray, 1870), p.7.
19. *Ibid.*, pp.26-7.
20. E.J. Willson, *Nurserymen to the World* (1989), pp.94-6.
21. S.H.M Frederick Street's diary, copy held.
22. *Camberley News*, 16 December 1916.
23. S.H.M. Heathermead file.
24. S.H.M. Harry Goold's reminiscences.
25. E.J. Willson, *Nurserymen to the World* (1989), p.102.
26. S.H.M. Reminiscences of Brian and Vic Berry.
27. S.H.M. Reminiscences of Bill Godfrey.
28. S.H.M. Reminiscences of Peter Higgs.
29. S.H.M. Reminiscences of Percy Small.
30. S.H.M. Reminiscences of Arthur Glazier.
31. S.H.M. Fenns Lane nursery file.

CHAPTER EIGHT – LARGE HOUSES AND ESTATES

1. Universal Directory (1791).
2. S.H.M. Lionel Parr's reminiscences.
3. S.H.M. Schueller Papers.
4. S.H.M. Frederick Street's diary.
5. Original held at Gordon's School; copy at S.H.M.
6. Ken Clarke, *The Royal Albert Orphanage and School*, Surrey Heath History Club (2004).
7. J.R. Bignall, *Frimley: The Biography of a Sanatorium* (Seven Corners Press, 1979).
8. S.H.M. Baldwin Brown file.
9. *May's Directory of Camberley* (1932).
10. 2 April 1926.
11. *The British Journal of Nursing*, 8 July 1916, p.36.
12. John Aubrey, *Natural History and Antiquities of the County of Surrey*, vol.3 (Kohler & Coombes, 1975), p.211.
13. S.H.M. Lewis file.
14. Longman, Green & Co. (1919).
15. Katherine Furse, *Hearts and Pomegranates* (1940).
16. Hamo Thorneycroft.

S.H.C. 361/15/3

The inhabitants of the Parish of Windlesham in the county of Surrey are intitled to Common in Gross in and upon the Waste Lands … commonly called Bagshot Heath which Are situate in the parish of Windlesham & have been used & accustomed to exercise their rights from time immemorial. The labouring Poor work thereon in digging sand and Gravel Stones & also in cutting Turves and digging peat as well for themselves as their neighbours Parishioners of the said Parish to whom they sell them at 18d & 2s per thousand to be consumed within the said Parish. The Ashes made by the Turves are used within the said Parish as Manure. Some of the poor pull heath for the purpose of making Brooms – a Manufactory of that sort being carried on at the Workhouse. Others cut heath for the Surveyors of the Parish to mend roads and various other purposes all tending to the Benefit of the Parish and according to the custom to be used within the Parish.

About 40 or 50 years ago a Kiln was erected for the purpose of burning Bricks, Tiles etc. which was afterwards removed to the place it now stands where it has continued undisturbed for 30 yrs past. The respective Occupiers of sd. Kiln have from time to time burnt their Bricks and Tiles with Faggots, Pollards and other Wood together with some Heath and Furze cut off from the sd. Waste Lands which has never been particularly noticed having been used in a moderate degree till within these few years when wood becoming very expensive – the present occupier Mr Henry Bartholomew has cut a much greater quantity of Heath to burn his Bricks Etc. than heretofore to the great injury of the Poor & other inhabitants of the sd. Parish in their respective Rights of Common & Turbary; the Cutting of the Heath totally spoiling the Turves for some years. In the beginning of last summer Mr Wm. Knight of Bagshot in the sd. Parish erected a new Kiln & for the space of 3 or 4 Months last past has employed many Men to cut Heath for the purpose of burning Bricks Tiles Lime etc. (having entered into a Contract with the Government to furnish out of the sd. Parish a given quantity thereof) to the destruction of the Turbary of the sd. Common & to the great Injury of the sd. Inhabitants & in all probability will tend to a great increase of the poor rates causing the poor to purchase Coal or some other fuel instead of having Turves at the expense of merely carting them.

The case was complicated by the fact that the title deeds to the land had been lost or mislaid and that the parishioners would have to prove their right to the traditional use of the land by using similar deeds owned by local farmers or possibly by calling elderly witnesses to confirm long-held practices. The land in Windlesham was divided into several Manorial holdings: Foster, Broomhall, Freemantle, Bagshot and Windlesham, each with a different lord of the manor, some of them owned by St John's College, Cambridge and with none of them resident it was more difficult in this village than in any of the others to be clear about the traditional rights to use of the land.

Appendix Two (Surrey Advertiser, August 1873)

The proposals it was thought would help to settle disputes between the interests of all parties were:

A) An Act of Parliament to be obtained providing:

1) For the abandonment by Lord Onslow of claims to dig for clay, stones and minerals, in the Commons, or so much thereof that remains unclosed after the Act, or to remove the surface of so much of the Common, with or without the consent of homage.
2) In consideration thereof, compensation to Lord Onslow, on liberal terms, by an allotment of an apportionment of the Common, such allotments to be held free and discharged of all common rights.
3) Confirmation of all existing enclosures – except Benham's which is to be abandoned.
4) Grants of land not yet enclosed to be separately dealt with, by return of the consideration money paid to the Lord.
5) Defendant and other brick makers to have liberty to work their kilns until 1st January 1875.

All terms of the above arrangement to be contingent on obtaining an Act of Parliament.

Appendix Three

Sir – What do the commoners want? Such was the question addressed to the meeting on Tuesday last by Mr Smallpiece, the Lord of the Manor's agent.

My reply is 'Chobham-Common' … I would however explain what the commoners do not want.

1) They don't want his Lordship either by himself or those to whom he may think fit to grant leave or licence to dig for brick earth, thereby destroying the herbage and turf on the common.
2) They don't want him to dig pits for clay, gravel or stones, close to the sides of the main roads, to a depth of six or eight feet, and leave them without protection whatever.
3) They don't want him to cut up the roads and cause heavy expenditure to repair the same, by the constant carting of brick earth, etc from the place where it is dug to the brick kilns, and by the carting of the bricks when burnt.
4) They don't want their fuel cut to burn in the said kilns thereby depriving the poor of their rights, which they want to exercise, and do exercise more than ever now that coal is so dear.
5) They don't want his Lordship to grant any portion of the common for enclosure, either for compensation or for loss sustained in defending any of his Lordship's claims, or for any other purpose whatsoever.
6) They don't want the green swards cut and carried away for the purpose of laying down lawns etc. between here and London, and elsewhere. I have letters here in my possession addressed to me, asking permission to cut the same to match those that have been cut on a previous occasion, and observing that it is hard that the party who resides in Addlestone should not be allowed to obtain them.
7) They don't want the top spit and fuel to be dug and carted away by gentlemen in neighbouring parishes, for the rearing of plants or the filling of holes in their domain.
8) They don't want persons from other parishes (where their common lands have been enclosed, and the parties or their predecessors compensated) to come and cut the turf or litter for their own profit and to the loss of the Commoners.

Index